The Words of
the Twelve Prophets

The Words of the Twelve Prophets

MESSAGES TO THE LATTER-DAY SAINTS

Monte S. Nyman
Farres H. Nyman

Deseret Book Company
Salt Lake City, Utah

Library of Congress Cataloging-in-Publication Data

Nyman, Monte S.
   The words of the twelve prophets : messages to the Latter-day Saints / by Monte S. Nyman and Farres H. Nyman.
      p.   cm.
   Includes bibliographical references.
   ISBN 0-87579-357-6
      1. Bible. O.T. Minor Prophets—Criticism, interpretation, etc.,
2. Mormon Church—Doctrines.   3. Church of Jesus Christ of Latter-day Saints—Doctrines.   I. Nyman, Farres H. II. Title.
BS1560.N95   1990
224'.906—dc20   90-34347
                                                                        CIP

Printed in the United States of America

10   9   8   7   6   5   4   3   2   1

Contents

Key to Abbreviations

CHC   Comprehensive History of the Church
CR   Conference Report
DS   Doctrines of Salvation
HC   History of the Church
JS—H   Joseph Smith—History
JS—M   Joseph Smith—Matthew
JST   Joseph Smith Translation of the Bible
JD   Journal of Discourses
KJV   King James Version of the Bible
MFP   Messages of the First Presidency
RSV   Revised Standard Version of the Bible
TPJS   Teachings of the Prophet Joseph Smith

The Words of the Twelve Prophets

The Savior admonished the Nephites to "search the prophets, for many there be that testify of these things" (3 Nephi 23:5). The "Prophets," as they were called in the ancient Hebrew canon of scripture, were divided into two segments: the former prophets and the later prophets. The former prophets constituted the books of Joshua, Judges, Samuel, and Kings (the latter two are now divided into 1 and 2 Samuel and 1 and 2 Kings). The later prophets were the books of Isaiah, Jeremiah, Ezekiel, and the Twelve,[1] which consisted of the last twelve books of the Old Testament in the present King James Version of the Bible. All the prophets were bound together as one book.

"These things" the prophets testified of were scriptures concerning the house of Israel. The Savior commanded the Nephites to search the words of Isaiah "diligently; for great are the words of Isaiah" (3 Nephi 23:1):

> For surely he spake as touching all things concerning my people which are of the house of Israel; therefore it must needs be that he must speak also to the Gentiles. And all things that he spake have been and shall be, even according to the words which he spake (3 Nephi 23:2–3).

---

[1] The book of Daniel was included in the "Hagiographa" or "the Writings," a third division of the Hebrew Bible. However, some comparisons to this great prophet are also included in this chapter.

1

Two Book of Mormon prophets also authenticated Jeremiah's works (1 Nephi 5:13; 7:14; Helaman 8:20). Modern revelation has confirmed the prophecies of Ezekiel (D&C 29:21) and Daniel (D&C 65:2, 6; 116; JS–M 1:12, 32). The validity of the books of the Twelve Prophets is implied in the Savior's admonition to "search the prophets."

Other Witnesses to Isaiah

Isaiah foretold the downfall of both houses of Israel. Many of the Twelve Prophets verify Isaiah's writings and serve as additional witnesses to the downfall of the Northern Ten Tribes of Israel in 722 B.C. Others of those Twelve Prophets serve as additional witnesses to Judah's downfall in 586 B.C. (traditional dating). Although three of these Twelve Prophets wrote after the fall of the two Israelite nations (Haggai, Zechariah, and Malachi), their messages are as pertinent to latter-day Israel as are Isaiah's and the other prophets' messages. As a further validation of these prophets' writings, the Savior commanded the Nephite record keepers to include much of Malachi's writings in the Book of Mormon (3 Nephi 24:1). The Savior also authenticated some of Zechariah's prophecies in a revelation given to Joseph Smith (D&C 45:51–53). The Lord has thus placed his stamp of approval firmly upon the writings of the Twelve Prophets.

The Greatness of the Prophets

The ancient prophets were great men, not only because they were prophets but also because they were prophets in a unique time and situation. They lived in a time when the gospel in its fulness and the Melchizedek Priesthood had been taken from the children of Israel (D&C 84:24–25) because "they were a stiffnecked people, quick to do iniquity, and slow to remember the Lord their God" (Mosiah 13:29). Their unique situation was that the law of Moses, which, according to the prophet Abinadi, was "a law of performances and of ordinances, a law which they were to observe strictly from day to day, to keep them in remembrance of God and their duty

2

towards him" (Mosiah 13:30), had been added to the gospel (*TPJS*, p. 160). These prophets demonstrated their greatness by rising above these obstacles and preparing themselves to receive the Melchizedek Priesthood so they could better serve the people. As the Prophet Joseph Smith taught:

> Was the Priesthood of Melchizedek taken away when Moses died? All Priesthood is Melchizedek, but there are different portions or degrees of it. That portion which brought Moses to speak with God face to face was taken away; but that which brought the ministry of angels [the Aaronic] remained (*TPJS*, pp. 180–81).

Then the prophet added parenthetically: "All the prophets had the Melchizedek Priesthood and were ordained by God himself" (*TPJS*, p. 181). This implies that these twelve did receive that further portion of the priesthood, which enabled them to see God face to face. It is also verified by the testimony of such prophets as Isaiah (6:1–4) and Ezekiel (1:26–3:14).

The Prophet's statement also teaches us that these prophets "were ordained by God himself." There are two important concepts in this statement. First, God foreordained these noble and great ones to come forth when they did so that they might fulfill a specific mission to the peoples of their time. This, of course, is confirmed by the Lord's statement to Jeremiah: "Before I formed thee in the belly I knew thee; and before thou camest forth out of the womb I sanctified thee, and I ordained thee a prophet unto the nations" (Jeremiah 1:5). This is also suggested in the calls given to other prophets, such as Amos (Amos 7:14–15). It was undoubtedly true of all the prophets (see *TPJS*, p. 365).

The second concept is that God himself ordained these twelve. Since ordaining a prophet is an earthly ordinance, these prophets were undoubtedly also ordained by a mortal representative of God upon the earth, but they were personally selected or designated by God for this sacred privilege of holding the Melchizedek Priesthood, having lived up to their premortal foreordination. Since all who

3

hold the Melchizedek Priesthood at any time are foreordained (Alma 13:1–5), this may not seem too significant; however, when one remembers the stiff-necked condition of the children of Israel at this time, the calling of these prophets becomes a great compliment to their dedication.

The importance of the prophets is further illustrated by the fact that their writings were a major source from which Jesus and the Apostles taught the gospel in the meridian of time. There are at least forty-two passages that can assuredly be identified as Isaiah's writings quoted in the New Testament. There are twenty-seven passages from the prophet Jeremiah that can positively be identified, and at least twenty-five passages from the Twelve Prophets. Several other passages may also be from the Twelve Prophets, but only the positively identified quotes are here counted. How many more passages were included before the many plain and precious parts were taken away (1 Nephi 13:24–29) can only be left to speculation, but there obviously were some, as shown by Matthew 27:9 and Helaman 8:19–20.

The Book of Mormon prophets also quoted extensively from these Old Testament prophets. At least 425 separate verses from Isaiah are quoted in the Book of Mormon. Ten verses from the prophet Micah are quoted by the Savior himself, several more than once. The Father commanded Jesus to quote the entire third and fourth chapters of Malachi as he ministered to the Nephites (3 Nephi 24–25). One verse from Habakkuk (3 Nephi 21:9) and possibly one from Hosea (Mosiah 16:7) are also quoted in the Book of Mormon. Because many of these prophets lived and testified after Lehi left Jerusalem, they are not more widely quoted in the Book of Mormon.

In addition, many prophecies of the prophets are included in the revelations to Joseph Smith, although they are not identified as being from those prophets. A careful analysis will disclose that at least seventy quotations from Isaiah, seven from Jeremiah, five from Ezekiel, nine from Daniel, and thirty-one from the Twelve Prophets are quoted in the Doctrine and Covenants. In working on

4

his inspired translation, the Prophet made extensive corrections in the writings of the later prophets. Of particular interest in this work are the twenty-two changes in the text of the Twelve Prophets.

Another Testament of Jesus Christ

One of the major reasons to search the prophets is to see the testimony that they bear of Jesus Christ. Nephi quoted Isaiah so that he "might more fully persuade [his people] to believe in the Lord their Redeemer" (1 Nephi 19:23). Jeremiah prophesied concerning the coming of the Son of God (Jeremiah 8:20). All of the prophets have written and prophesied concerning the Christ (Jacob 4:4; 7:11). The Twelve Prophets were among all those who testified of the Savior, as their written records will attest.

The Fulfillment of the Prophets

Another reason for studying the prophets is that their writings are being fulfilled in our day. As the Savior ministered among the Nephites, he made this informative declaration:

> Behold, I say unto you that the law is fulfilled that was given unto Moses.
>
> Behold, I am he that gave the law, and I am he who covenanted with my people Israel; therefore, the law in me is fulfilled, for I have come to fulfill the law; therefore it hath an end.
>
> *Behold, I do not destroy the prophets, for as many as have not been fulfilled in me, verily I say unto you, shall all be fulfilled.*
>
> And because I said unto you that old things have passed away, *I do not destroy that which hath been spoken concerning things which are to come.*
>
> For behold, the covenant which I have made with my people is not all fulfilled; but the law which was given unto Moses hath an end in me.
>
> Behold, I am the law, and the light. Look unto me, and endure to the end, and ye shall live; for unto him that endureth to the end will I give eternal life (3 Nephi 15:4–9; italics added).

5

Since this statement was made following the Savior's ministry among the Jews, and because there was a long period of apostasy following his ministry and the ministry of his chosen apostles in Jerusalem, it is obvious that the prophets' prophecies were directed to the Restoration in the latter days. This is supported by the Prophet Joseph Smith:

> The time has at last arrived when the God of Abraham, of Isaac, and of Jacob, has set his hand again the second time to recover the remnants of his people, which have been left from Assyria, and from Egypt, and from Pathros, and from Cush, and from Elam, and from Shinar, and from Hamath, and from the islands of the sea, and with them to bring in the fulness of the Gentiles, and establish that covenant with them, which was promised when their sins should be taken away. See Isaiah xi; Romans xi:25, 26 and 27, and also Jeremiah xxxi:31, 32 and 33. This covenant has never been established with the house of Israel, nor with the house of Judah, for it requires two parties to make a covenant, and those two parties must be agreed, or no covenant can be made.
>
> Christ, in the days of His flesh, proposed to make a covenant with them, but they rejected Him and His proposals, and in consequence thereof, they were broken off, and no covenant was made with them at that time. But their unbelief has not rendered the promise of God of none effect; no, for there was another day limited in David, which was the day of His power; and then His people, Israel, should be a willing people; — and He would write His law in their hearts, and print it in their thoughts; their sins and their iniquities He would remember no more.
>
> Thus after this chosen family had rejected Christ and His proposals, the heralds of salvation said to them, "Lo we turn unto the Gentiles" and the Gentiles received the covenant, and were grafted in from whence the chosen family were broken off; but the Gentiles have not continued in the goodness of God, but have departed from the faith that was once delivered to the Saints, and have broken the covenant in which their fathers were established (see Isaiah xxiv:5); and have become high-minded, and have not

feared; therefore, but few of them will be gathered with the chosen family. Have not the pride, high-mindedness, and unbelief of the Gentiles, provoked the Holy One of Israel to withdraw His Holy Spirit from them, and send forth His judgments to scourge them for their wickedness? This is certainly the case (*TPJS*, pp. 14–15).

The Savior also taught that when the words of Isaiah should be fulfilled, then the covenant the Father made unto the house of Israel would be fulfilled (3 Nephi 16:17; 20:11–12). This covenant was originally made with Abraham and passed on through Isaac and Jacob, whose name was changed to Israel. That the covenant of Abraham is being fulfilled today through The Church of Jesus Christ of Latter-day Saints is confirmed repeatedly in the Doctrine and Covenants (D&C 103:17; 124:58; 132:30–32). The prophets had this fulfillment in mind as they prophesied centuries ago.

The Prophets Warn the Nations

The prophets followed a pattern of proclaiming a message of doom to their present society but always ending with a pronouncement of hope. The message of hope was centered in the last days when a remnant of Israel would be restored to their promised lands and blessings. The specific messages of each prophet will be covered in the appropriate chapters of this book. For now, an overview of the historical setting and prophecies for the future will suffice to illustrate this concept.

Many of the prophets ministered around the time of the Assyrian captivity of the ten and one-half tribes of Israel. This period, from approximately 800 to 700 B.C., was the time of the prophet Isaiah. Micah, Hosea, and Amos were other witnesses against the wickedness that led to the destruction and captivity of the northern nation of Palestine, and they are thus called the eighth-century prophets. Joel, Obadiah, and Jonah probably also prophesied during this period, but their dating is controversial. All of these prophets carry a unique message as well as confirm what Isaiah had declared.

Hosea foretells the latter-day gathering of the house of Israel in the context of strange marriages and gives special emphasis to Ephraim. Joel speaks of the Spirit being poured out upon all flesh (which the angel Moroni said was soon to be fulfilled) and describes the Gentiles gathered together against the Jews in the valley of decision. After chastising Israel for their social sins, Amos predicts the latter-day famine of the Lord's word and the restoration of those who have been sifted as corn among all the nations of the earth. Obadiah's writings are not lengthy; however, to him is ascribed the commonly known phrase and prophecy that "saviours shall come up on mount Zion" (Obadiah 1:21). Jonah's great message of God's love for all people is certainly applicable to us in this day of racial strife. Micah adds his warning of the Lamanites treading down the Gentiles who do not repent in the latter days.

The next time period of the prophets is the Babylonian captivity of Jerusalem, with many Jews being carried into exile in Babylon (607 B.C. is the traditional biblical dating). The prophets Ezekiel and Daniel were raised up unto those captive peoples to guide them while separated from their homeland. Ezekiel's extensive visions included the restoration of the two nations of the house of Israel — Judah (Southern Israel) and Ephraim (Northern Israel) — to one fold under one shepherd through the coming forth of the Book of Mormon. He also foresaw many other aspects of the last days, including the great battle of Gog and Magog. Daniel interpreted King Nebuchadnezzar's dream showing the kingdom of God being set up on the earth in the latter days and also that kingdom being prepared and presented to the Son of Man by Adam, the Ancient of Days.

Before and after the Jewish exiles were taken away, prophets throughout the land of Judah warned them of Babylon's oncoming invasion. Foremost among these prophets was the oft-persecuted Jeremiah. His life was a prime example of the Savior's declaration to the Jewish people that "so persecuted they the prophets who were before you" (Matthew 5:12). Jeremiah's "many prophecies," as labeled by Nephi, included several that are being fulfilled in our day. The Lord is taking "one of a city, and two of a family" and bringing them to Zion (Jeremiah 3:14). He is also sending for many fishers and many hunters to accomplish a greater gathering than when the children of Israel were brought out of Egypt (Jeremiah 16:14–16). The new covenant has been made with the house of Israel and will undoubtedly soon be made with the house of Judah, as Jeremiah prophesied (Jeremiah 31:31–34). The prophets Habakkuk and Zephaniah were also prophesying during this same time period (approximately 630–580 B.C.). Habakkuk foretold a marvelous work to come forth among the Gentiles in the latter days. We can turn to Zephaniah to learn of events preceding the Lord's second coming and of the return of a pure language to the Lord's people (Zephaniah 3:1–9).

The writings of the prophets are then silent for a brief time, until the decree of Cyrus allowed the Jews to return to their beloved homeland (538 B.C. is the traditional date of the decree). The Lord then raises up two prophets, Haggai and Zechariah, to inspire the people to rebuild the city and the holy temple. While Haggai's message is basically to inspire his people to build a temple, he does speak of the coming Messiah, "the desire of all nations" (Haggai 2:7). Such is not the case with Zechariah; his message extends to both comings of Jesus Christ and graphically predicts the Messiah's appearance to the Jews when all nations are gathered against the latter-day nations of Judah (Zechariah 12:9–10; 14:1–9).

The last of the prophets comes to us again after a long, dry spell of no writings (about 400 B.C.). Malachi, however, does not leave us wanting for prophecies about the latter days. Latter-day Saints are thrilled with his prophetic utterances of the messenger of the covenant to precede the Lord's coming in judgment upon the world, of his promise and warnings to latter-day Israel regarding the payment of tithes and offerings, and of the necessity of the coming of Elijah (which coming they joyfully announce has taken place). There are also other choice tidbits within his writings for those who will search the prophets.

The Text and the Times of the Prophets

In spite of these many reasons for searching the prophets, many people are discouraged from reading the Old Testament because of its length, because of its difficulty, and because they don't know the history and the background of the peoples. Perhaps a few facts will allay at least some of their fears and give them encouragement to read again. The new Church publication of the Bible contains 1,184 pages in the Old Testament; 860 of these pages precede the writings of the prophets. This leaves only 324 pages of writings of the prophets from Isaiah to Malachi, which include many footnotes and cross-references, thus making even fewer pages of actual writings. This may not seem too significant until it is realized that the New Testament, again including footnotes and cross-references, contains 403 pages. This means that there are 79 fewer pages in the writings of the prophets than in the New Testament; thus, the prophets are only 80 percent of the length of the New Testament. Furthermore, although Isaiah and his contemporaries began their work after 800 B.C., the actual time comprising their writings is brief.

There are two major time periods of only fifty to one hundred years each that include all but the last three of the sixteen prophets' writings included in the present-day Bible. Looked at in this way, becoming acquainted with the historical and cultural backgrounds of these two brief time periods should not be overly difficult. This task should be enhanced by a knowledge of the great rewards that will follow such a study. These two time periods should be of special interest to Latter-day Saints because of their relevance to us as a people. The first, the time preceding and following the taking away of the ten tribes, is the history of our ancestors. Ephraim was the birthright tribe and therefore the spiritual leader of the house of Israel. After the division of the two nations, following the reign of Solomon, the northern nation was known and called by the name of Ephraim. As the ten tribes were taken into the north, Ephraim particularly was scattered among the nations of the earth and today is being gathered out. A study of this time period is a study of our people.

The second time period is of equal importance. During this approximately fifty-year period, the prophet Lehi was called out of Jerusalem; he and his partner in travel, Ishmael, represent both tribes of Joseph—Manasseh and Ephraim—to whom this great land of the Americas was given (3 Nephi 15:12–13). The land they left and the land to which they traveled constitute the two lands of promise where the house of Israel will be gathered. The background of Palestine acquaints us with the prophecies regarding the future gathering to that land. Members of the Church are primarily of the blood of Ephraim. As the birthright holder, Ephraim is responsible for the gathering of the ten thousands of Ephraim and the thousands of Manasseh upon the American continent (Deuteronomy 33:15–17; compare D&C 58:44–45). The Prophet Joseph Smith taught:

> You know there has been great discussion in relation to Zion—where it is, and where the gathering of the dispensation is, and which I am now going to tell you. The prophets have spoken and written upon it; but I will make a proclamation that will cover a broader ground. The whole of America is Zion itself from north to south, and is described by the Prophets, who declare that it is the Zion where the mountain of the Lord should be, and that it should be in the center of the land. When Elders shall take up and examine the old prophecies in the Bible, they will see it (*TPJS*, p. 362).

Thus the second time period should also have a special interest to us in the latter days.

The brief time periods of Haggai, Zechariah, and Malachi may not be as significant to our day historically, but their writings certainly do contain, as previously stated, prophecies of this latter day that are just as significant doctrinally to us.

Conclusion

If we will keep the commandment to search the prophecies of Isaiah and also these other prophets, we will come to agree with Jesus' pronouncement that "great are the words of Isaiah" and that

11

"many there be that testify of these things" (3 Nephi 23:1–6). The following chapters are designed to help Latter-day Saints understand the specific messages of the Twelve Prophets and how they are being fulfilled in our day. For specific discussions of the books of Isaiah and Jeremiah, see *Great Are the Words of Isaiah* (Salt Lake City: Bookcraft, 1980) and *The Words of Jeremiah* (Salt Lake City: Bookcraft, 1982).

CHAPTER 2

The Eighth-Century Prophets

The kingdom of Northern Israel, also known as Ephraim, came to an end in the year 721 B.C. Hoshea, their last king, had become the puppet king of Shalmaneser, king of Assyria, the world power. Because Hoshea failed to pay his tribute money and had conspired with So, the king of Egypt, Shalmaneser imprisoned Hoshea and besieged Samaria, the capital of Israel, for three years. Many of the surviving Israelites were carried back into Assyria (2 Kings 17:2–6). Shalmaneser then brought people from Babylon and other Gentile nations to inhabit the land (2 Kings 17:24). This was the beginning of the nation of the Samaritans.

The historical background of Israel's fall is recorded in 1 and 2 Kings. The actual fall is recorded in 2 Kings 17. While these chapters contain other incidents of historical or doctrinal interest, we will examine only those pertaining to Israel's downfall. Because these chapters are an abridgment of a more extensive record (see 2 Kings 10:34; 13:8, 12; 14:28; 15:11, 15, 21, 26, 31), they do not contain many details. However, they do lay the groundwork for an understanding of the Lord's involvement in Israel's fall. They illustrate the positive answer to the Lord's question to modern-day Israel, the Latter-day Saints: "Do I not hold the destinies of all the armies of the nations of the earth?" (D&C 17:6.) They further give the setting of the words or messages of the prophets of this time period.

The messages of the prophets are based upon principles determined by the Lord. Since the brief record of 1 and 2 Kings does not outline these principles, we must turn elsewhere to learn them. The Book of Mormon teaches three great principles that are applicable to the work and messages of the prophets of this time period. They are: (1) the Lord destroys a nation when it is ripened in iniquity; (2) the Lord never destroys a nation unless he first warns it by the prophets; and (3) the Lord leads the more righteous out before he destroys the nations of the wicked. These three principles warrant a close look in order to appreciate their value in relation to the prophets discussed in this book.

A Nation Ripened in Iniquity

In speaking of the inhabitants of the land of Canaan before the Lord brought the children of Israel out of Egypt, Nephi declared: "Behold, the Lord esteemeth all flesh in one; he that is righteous is favored of God. But behold, this people had rejected every word of God, and they were ripe in iniquity; and the fulness of the wrath of God was upon them; and the Lord did curse the land against them, and bless it unto our fathers; yea, he did curse it against them unto their destruction, and he did bless it unto our fathers unto their obtaining power over it" (1 Nephi 17:35).

The Bible confirms this principle. The Lord told Abram (Abraham) that the Amorites would not be driven out of the land that the Lord had given him until four hundred years hence because their iniquity was "not yet full" (Genesis 15:13–16). When Joshua entered the land of Canaan, the four hundred years' waiting time was fulfilled.

In the eighth century B.C., the nation of Israel was also ripe in iniquity and thus ready for destruction at the hands of the Lord. This is verified by the description in scripture of the leadership of the people. The record of 1 and 2 Kings lists nineteen kings of Israel. The abridger labels all nineteen of them as evil in the sight of the Lord. These kings ruled about two hundred and fifty years in total. By contrast, most of the kings of Judah during this same period

14

were designated as doing right in the sight of the Lord (see the chart at the end of this chapter). The Lord has revealed that "when the wicked rule the people mourn" (D&C 98:9; Proverbs 29:2). Further, in the words of Mosiah, "the sins of many people have been caused by the iniquities of their kings" (Mosiah 29:31; see also 29:17 and 23:9).

That the people followed the examples of their evil kings is testified of in the summation in 2 Kings 17 of why Israel fell: the children of Israel sinned against the Lord their God. They walked in the statutes of the heathens, whom the Lord cast out before the children of Israel. Furthermore, they secretly built high places for worship in all their cities and set up "images and groves in every high hill, and under every green tree." They "burnt incense in all the high places, as did the heathen whom the Lord carried away before them." Therefore they "served idols," which the Lord had said they should not do (2 Kings 17:7–12). These abominations and iniquities of the kings and the people faced the prophets as they testified to Israel.

The Lord Warns by the Prophets

Speaking concerning the Jews, Nephi testified: "As one generation hath been destroyed among the Jews because of iniquity, even so have they been destroyed from generation to generation according to their iniquities; and never hath any of them been destroyed save it were foretold them by the prophets of the Lord" (2 Nephi 25:9).

The Lord followed this principle in dealing with the nations of Israel and Judah. The book of Kings records: "Yet the Lord testified against Israel, and against Judah, by all the prophets, and by all the seers, saying, Turn ye from your evil ways, and keep my commandments and my statutes, according to all the law which I commanded your fathers, and which I sent to you by my servants the prophets" (2 Kings 17:13).

The text continues that Israel "would not hear, but hardened their necks," like "their fathers, that did not believe in the Lord

15

their God. And they rejected his statutes, and his covenants that he made with their fathers, and his testimonies [of the prophets] which he testified against them" (2 Kings 17:14–15). They worshiped all the host of heaven and served the pagan god Baal, which included images of golden calves, temple prostitution in the groves, sacrifice of their children to the god Molech, divination, and enchantments. For these grievous sins, the nation of Israel was moved out of the Lord's sight. She was allowed to be afflicted and spoiled by the hand of Assyria. She had followed the sins of idolatry and priestcraft established by their first king, Jeroboam (2 Kings 17:20–24; compare 1 Kings 12:25–33). The Lord followed the principle taught by Mormon (Mormon 4:5) — the wicked (Israel) were punished by the wicked (Assyria). Only the nation of Judah was left in the promised land (2 Kings 17:14–18). Although she did not keep the commandments of the Lord as she should, she did keep the statutes or covenants she had made (2 Kings 17:19). She had not rejected the prophets as had Israel.

The book of 2 Kings mentions only one of the prophets whose writings have been preserved, that of Jonah, the son of Amittai (2 Kings 14:25; Jonah 1:1). The chronology chart in the Bible Dictionary contained in the LDS version of the King James edition of the Bible (1979) shows the traditional dating of the other prophets whose writings have been preserved. These would include Hosea, Joel, Amos, Isaiah, and Micah. Obadiah probably testified during this time also. There may have been others as well. Earlier chapters of 1 and 2 Kings refer to several prophets who testified to Israel but whose writings we do not have. Chief among these were Elijah (1 Kings 17–2 Kings 2) and Elisha (1 Kings 19:25–31; 2 Kings 2–13). Others mentioned include Ahijah, Iddo, and Shemaiah (1 Kings 11:29–39; 12:15; 14:2–16; 15:29; 2 Chronicles 9:29; 12:15). Either these prophets did not record their messages or through the loss of "plain and precious parts" they are no longer in our Bible (1 Nephi 13:23–29).

The Lord warned the people of Israel before they were destroyed.

Many of the people were undoubtedly killed, but the Lord preserved others by removing them to another land (2 Kings 17:18, 23).

The Righteous Led into Precious Lands

Returning to Nephi's prophecy of the inhabitants of the land of Canaan at the time the Lord led Israel out of Egypt, we learn the third great principle concerning the destruction of the nation of Israel: "He raiseth up a righteous nation, and destroyeth the nations of the wicked. And he leadeth away the righteous into precious lands, and the wicked he destroyeth, and curseth the land unto them for their sakes" (1 Nephi 17:37–38).

The Lord led Israel into the land of Assyria and later took them into the land of the North. He also scattered them among all the nations of the earth. The prophets of the Old Testament not only foretold these events but also gave the reasons for this scattering and the promises of their latter-day gathering.

The removal of Israel had been prophesied "by all [the Lord's] servants the prophets" (2 Kings 17:23). There are two parts of those prophecies. First, the prophet Amos foretold that the Lord would not destroy all the house of Israel but would scatter them "among all nations" (Amos 9:8–9). This was apparently fulfilled at least partially as the ten tribes were taken into Assyria and the North. The other part of the prophecy was their going as a body into the North. In the Apocrypha, we read this interesting account of

> the ten tribes which were led away from their own land into captivity in the days of King Hoshea, whom Shalmaneser the king of the Assyrians led captive; he took them across the river, and they were taken into another land. But they formed this plan for themselves, that they would leave the multitude of the nations and go to a more distant region, where mankind had never lived, that there at least they might keep their statutes which they had not kept in their own land. And they went in by the narrow passages of the Euphrates river. For at that time the Most High performed signs for them, and stopped the channels of the river until they had passed over. Through that region

17

there was a long way to go, a journey of a year and a half; and that country is called Arzareth.

Then they dwelt there until the last times; and now, when they are about to come again, the Most High will stop the channels of the river again, so that they may be able to pass over. Therefore, you saw the multitude gathered together in peace. But those who are left of your people, who are found within my holy borders, shall be saved (2 Esdras 14:40–48).

The first part of the prophecies, their being scattered among all nations, is being constantly verified today through patriarchal blessings given to members of the Church as they are converted to the gospel from the many nations of the world. The second part of the prophecy, their going as a body into the North, is evidenced by the Savior's declaration to the Nephites that he was going to visit them in the meridian of time (3 Nephi 15:15; 16:1–3; 17:4).

Although it was among the plain and precious parts that were lost from the Old Testament, another prophecy was fulfilled when Assyria captured Northern Israel. The allegory of Zenos, retained for us in the Book of Mormon (Jacob 5), foretold the grafting of the Gentile branches into the trunk of the olive tree representing the house of Israel. This grafting was accomplished when the king of Assyria brought men from Babylon and other nations into Israel (2 Kings 17:24). These men intermarried with a remnant of Israel that was left behind, culminating this Gentile graft. The interesting account of the trouble these grafted nations had with lions sent by the Lord — which resulted in one of the priests being sent back from Assyria to teach them "how they should fear the Lord" (2 Kings 17:25–28) — shows how this merger was affected to produce the good fruit as prophesied in the allegory (Jacob 5:17–18; compare John 4:27–42). The Lord works in mysterious ways to accomplish his design for his children.

That those taken into Assyria by the king were of the more righteous people of the northern Israelites is evidenced by the quotation from 2 Esdras above. These people were one of the branches of Israel planted in a nethermost part of the vineyard (Jacob 5:20). From them came the basis of the latter-day gathering.

Many of the prophets foretold the Lord's promise to restore a remnant of Israel in the latter days (for example, see Isaiah 1:9; 6:13; 10:20–22). This promise is being fulfilled today in the gathering of the blood of Israel from among the Gentiles and will be completed with the return of the ten tribes (2 Nephi 29:11–14; D&C 133:26–34).[1] The righteous of Northern Israel were preserved so that the Lord may set his hand a second time to restore the preserved of Israel (Isaiah 11:11–12).

Conclusion

The eternal principles of the Lord are seen in his work with the nation of Israel in the eighth century B.C. When a nation is ripe in iniquity, the Lord will allow other nations of the earth to destroy even his covenant people. However, he will not allow this to happen unless he first forewarns them by his servants the prophets. Being destroyed as a nation does not imply the destruction of the entire population. The Lord will preserve the more righteous of the nation by leading them out of their wicked environment and scattering them or establishing them in another land. After this scattering, the Lord will gather their posterity and renew his covenant with them. Thus, the Lord does "hold the destinies of all the armies of the nations of the earth" (D&C 117:6).

---

[1]For a more complete analysis of this, see Nyman, *An Ensign to All People* (Salt Lake City: Deseret Book Company, 1987), chapter 8.

Kings of Israel

Saul
David
Solomon

Kings of Northern Israel	Label of the Book of Kings	Kings of Judah	Label of the Book of Kings
Jeroboam (22)*	Evil	Rehoboam (17)	Evil
		Abijam (3)	Evil
		Asa (41)	Right
Nadab (2)	Evil		
Baasha (24)	Evil		
Elah (2)	Evil		
Zimri (7 days)			
Omri (12)	Evil	Jehosophat (25)	Right
Ahab (22)	Evil		
Ahaziah (2)	Evil		
Jehoram or Joran (12)	Evil	Jehoram or Joram (8)	Evil
		Ahaziah (1)	Evil
		Athaliah (6)	?
Jehu (28)	Evil		
		Joash or Jehoash (40)	Right
Jehoahaz (17)	Evil		
Jehoash (16)	Evil	Amaziah (29)	Right
Jeroboam II (41)	Evil		
		Azariah (Uzziah) (52)	Right
Zachariah (6 months)	Evil		
Menahem (10)	Evil		
Pekahiah (2)	Evil		
Pekah (20)	Evil		

Kings of Northern Israel	Label of the Book of Kings	Kings of Judah	Label of the Book of Kings
		Jotham (16)	Right
Hoshea (9)	Evil		
		Ahaz (16)	Evil
		Hezekiah (29)	Right
		Manasseh (55)	Evil
		Amon (2)	Evil
		Josiah (31)	Right
		Jehoahaz (3 months)	?
		Jehoiakim (11)	Evil
		Jehoiachin (3 months)	Evil
		Zedekiah (11)	Evil

722 - Assyrian Captivity   589 - Babylonian Captivity

*number in brackets = years reigned based on biblical text

21

Hosea – The Prophet of the Scattering and Gathering of Ephraim

The interest and the analysis of the book of Hosea has almost always focused on the strange marriage or marriages that it records. While the marriages are an interesting problem, to focus on them is to miss, in my opinion, the book's major message. For this reason, the title of this chapter focuses on the overall message rather than on such usual titles as "Hosea, Prophet of Love."[1] An understanding of the message is enhanced by knowing the historical setting of the prophet's life.

The book's introduction or superscription[2] indicates that Hosea lived "in the days of Uzziah, Jotham, Ahaz, and Hezekiah, kings of Judah, and in the days of Jeroboam, the son of Joash, king of Israel" (Hosea 1:1). The last year of Uzziah's reign is now fairly well agreed upon as being 740 B.C. Uzziah was appointed king of Israel in the twenty-seventh year of Jeroboam's forty-one year reign; therefore, Uzziah reigned only about fifteen years of his fifty-two-

---

[1]This title, taken from *The Voice of Israel's Prophets*, by Dr. Sidney B. Sperry (Salt Lake City: Deseret Book Company, 1952), is typical of the various books and chapters on Hosea.

[2]A superscription as used here is the introductory comments that were anciently used as headings to a book or sections of a book. They are used extensively in the Book of Mormon and are a part of the text from the plates of Nephi or Mormon; for example, the first paragraph of 1 Nephi, 2 Nephi, Jacob, and so on, and above Alma chapters 5, 7, 9, 17, and others. This is typical of ancient Hebrew writing and of the Old Testament, but modern translations have incorporated the superscriptions into the first verse of the first chapter.

year reign while Jeroboam was king of Israel and about thirty-seven years after Jeroboam died. Since Hosea prophesied during Jeroboam's reign, we can determine that his ministry likely began by 777 B.C. by adding these thirty-seven years of Uzziah's reign following Jeroboam's death to 740 B.C. Since Hosea began his ministry during the fifteen years that Uzziah and Jeroboam both reigned, we can date the beginning of Hosea's ministry between 777 and 791 B.C. He therefore preceded but overlapped Isaiah's ministry, which began in the last year of Uzziah's reign and extended until the death of Hezekiah.

Hosea prophesied until during Hezekiah's reign as king of Judah. The death of Hezekiah is traditionally accepted as 697 B.C. Since Hezekiah reigned for twenty-nine years, he began about 726 B.C. Hosea would therefore have prophesied until after 726 B.C. From before 777 B.C. until after 726 B.C. totals more than fifty years. All of this fifty-year period was the era of great wickedness before the downfall of Northern Israel, to whom Hosea's message seems to be addressed. His account begins with his being commanded to marry a wife of whoredoms.

Hosea's Marriages and Children

The various interpretations of the marriage described in Hosea 1:2–3 have been well summarized by Dr. Sidney B. Sperry:

> Views of capable commentators have been very diverse, but for convenience we may classify them under four heads:
>
> 1. The story is an allegory or parable symbolizing the relation existing between Jehovah and his people, Israel.
>
> 2. The story is assumed to be a literal account of actual facts. Many ancient interpreters took this position, and several modern critics have presented the view with considerable force and ingenuity.
>
> 3. The modified literal theory assumes that Gomer, Hosea's wife, was not a common harlot, but rather a Baal worshiper who was, therefore, guilty of spiritual harlotry. She may have even been a priestess of the cult, who had sacrificed her physical as well as her spiritual chastity by

reason of her fanatic devotion to it. Hosea could not, therefore, bring charges against her or have her put to death, because her position was considered honorable or sacred at the time. By ingenious interpretation or emendation of the text of Hosea 3:2, those who hold to this theory claim that what Hosea did was to pay Gomer's vow or debt to the shrine to which she resorted, and then bring her home and isolate her.

4. Many, if not most, modern expositors hold the view that Gomer was a pure woman when Hosea married her, and continued so until after the birth of her first child. (Sperry, p. 290.)

Regardless of whether this is a literal account of Hosea's marriage, it is symbolic of the marriage of Jehovah to Israel, as an analysis of the text regarding the children of the marriage will illustrate. Perhaps it was both literal and symbolic, Hosea's marriage serving as an object lesson to Israel.

The first son born to Gomer and Hosea was named Jezreel by the Lord. The meaning of the name was to "avenge the blood of Jezreel" (Hosea 1:4) and symbolizes the destruction of Northern Israel, the ten and one-half tribes taken into captivity by Assyria. Jezreel was the prominent valley of Northern Israel where Jehu had killed the sons of Ahab, the wicked king of Israel (2 Kings 10:11).

While Ahab had served the pagan god Baal, God had used Jehu to punish him and his house for their wicked practices, but Jehu had not walked "in the law of the Lord God of Israel" and "departed not from the sins of Jeroboam"[3] in worshiping Baal (2 Kings 10:30–31).

The worship of Baal included the sacrifice of little children, as well as other atrocities. The prophecy of Hosea represented in the first child of this marriage was, therefore, that Northern Israel was ripening in iniquity and would soon be destroyed.

---

[3]The Jeroboam referred to in 2 Kings 10:31 is the king who first reigned over Northern Israel when the kingdom was divided following Solomon's reign. It was he who introduced the worship of Baal. While this pagan worship flourished more at some times than others, it finally led to the downfall of the nation.

This prophecy is Hosea's first prophecy of the scattering of Ephraim, another name for the Northern Kingdom of Israel. The downfall to the Assyrians (721 B.C.) was to take place in the famous valley of Jezreel (Hosea 1:5). The blood that had been previously shed there in wickedness was apparently crying unto the Lord for justice (see 2 Nephi 28:10; D&C 136:36; Genesis 4:10). But Ephraim's doom was more involved.

The second child born to Hosea and Gomer was a daughter (Hosea 1:6–7). God commanded that she be named Lo-ruhamah. The name means, as the text states, that God will no longer extend mercy to the nation of Israel but will take them away. The first name-prophecy had foretold their downfall as a nation, and this name-prophecy adds the dimension of some of them being taken into captivity. The prophecy also extends mercy to the nation of Judah, who is not in the state of wickedness that her sister nation is.

The third child of the prophet and his wife was a boy. The child's name was to be Lo-ammi, which signifies that Israel is no longer recognized as the Lord's people (Hosea 1:8–9). He will no longer be their God. Jehovah had promised Moses in Egypt that Israel would be his people and that he would be their God (Exodus 6:7). He was now rescinding that covenant because Israel had not lived up to its conditional agreements (Deuteronomy 4:25–28; see also D&C 56:3–4). The Lord had destroyed them as a nation, taken them into captivity, and rejected them as his people, but, as Moses had also foretold, the Lord would yet extend them mercy (Deuteronomy 4:29–31).

The Message of Hope – A Latter-day Gathering

In the typical Old Testament prophets' pattern, the Lord gives Hosea a message of hope following a message of doom. This message introduces the concept of Israel's future gathering. God's covenant with Abraham was that his offspring would be as numberless as the sand of the sea (Genesis 22:17). The Lord here affirms, through Hosea, that this promise to Abraham is still in effect and will yet be fulfilled in spite of their destruction and captivity (Hosea 1:10). Israel, who were told that they are not God's people, will again be gathered and told they are the sons of the living God. This promise constitutes a restoration of the gospel and the authority to perform ordinances. Becoming the son or daughter of the living God comes through the ordinance of water baptism and the baptism of fire and the Holy Ghost, or spiritual adoption (Mosiah 5:7).

The prophecy also expands to include Judah. When Israel is gathered again, Judah will be likewise gathered, and the kingdom will be divided no longer. They will be under one head or government, the kingdom of God (Hosea 1:11). Paul recognized this as a prophecy to the Gentiles as well (Romans 9:26). Since Israel was to be scattered among the Gentiles, they would eventually be gathered out. The gathering from other lands will be a great day for Jezreel, or the nation of Israel.

Having foretold the scattering and promised gathering in chapter 1, chapter 2 describes this gathering from their scattered conditions among the Gentiles. The children are now designated as Ammi and Ruhamah. The *Lo*, which means "no" in Hebrew, is dropped. The Lord is saying that the children of Israel are once again to be his people and obtain mercy. Those who are called his people and have obtained mercy are to plead with their mother (Hosea 2:2).

This seems to refer to those of Israel who are gathered and then given the responsibility to gather the rest of the house of Israel. It is the same message recorded in Isaiah 52:11, the calling of Israel from among the Gentiles: "Depart ye, depart ye, go ye out from thence, touch no unclean thing; go ye out of the midst of her; be ye clean, that bear the vessels of the Lord."

It also carries the same message as another prophecy of Isaiah (49:3, 6). The people of Israel, as the gathered servant, are to raise up the tribes of Jacob and restore the preserved of Israel (among the Gentiles). As they are gathering the preserved of Israel, they will also give the Gentiles an opportunity to be numbered with Israel and further fulfill the Lord's covenant to Abraham that his seed would bless the nations of the Gentiles (Genesis 12:3). Thus, in

26

the context of Hosea, Ammi and Ruhamah represent the small gathered remnant children who are to plead with the mother of Israel, representing the vast number of the body of Israel.

Mother Israel is invited by the Lord to forsake her unfaithful practices that labeled her a harlot — the worshiping of other gods or symbolically having an affair with someone other than her husband, Jehovah (Hosea 2:2–5). Because Israel has followed other gods, she will not prosper and shall fail to find satisfaction in spiritual endeavors of these other gods. This will cause her to turn to her first husband, Jehovah, but she will have a period in which she will not prosper (Hosea 1:6–13).

Following this unprosperous period, the Lord will bring Israel into the wilderness and speak to her or gather her and give her revelation. At that day, Israel will recognize the Lord as her husband ("Ishi," see footnote to Hosea 2:16) and not call upon the names of Baalim (Hosea 2:14–17). The Lord will bless Israel and reinstate his marriage, and she shall know the Lord. God will again have mercy on Israel and be her God, and Israel will recognize him as her God (Hosea 2:18–23).

The gathering of Israel following the scattering is thus foretold through Hosea. This interpretation is strengthened through Paul's quoting of Hosea 2:23 as a promise to be fulfilled to the Gentiles (Romans 9:25). But the Lord has still more to say through Hosea concerning his marriage to Israel.

Chapter 3 is considered by many as a second marriage that Hosea is commanded to enter. In my opinion, it is not a second marriage but the lesson given to Hosea concerning the first marriage. It is the symbolic representation or application he is to follow. Hosea's command to love an adulteress who looks to other gods is an admonition for him to love Israel and teach the people as long as anyone will listen to him (Hosea 3:1). The purchase of the woman for certain amounts of silver and barley is symbolic of the Lord's taking his people out of their adulterous situation and placing them in another environment, not with him but away from Baal where they could not play the harlot by false worship (Hosea 3:2). The value of the silver and barley has been explained in various ways, but none of the explanations, to my knowledge, has been confirmed by revelation. There is undoubtedly some significance attached to the total price that will someday be understood and probably relates to the cost of redeeming Israel.

Since Israel has been purchased by the Lord, it is now his prerogative to do with her as he sees appropriate. Her punishment is set. She is to be taken away where she cannot worship Baal (Hosea 3:3). This was fulfilled by her being taken into captivity by Assyria and then allowed to go into the North (2 Esdras 14:40–48).

In this scattered condition, Israel would abide many days without a king, a prince, a sacrifice, an image, an ephod, and a teraphim (Hosea 3:4). This is another way of saying that the people will have no priesthood or political leadership from Christ, no ordinances or spiritual leadership of the church, and no revelation. The ephod and teraphim were instruments associated with revelation. In other words, Israel would be in a state of apostasy for many days.

Again, the prophecy ends with a message of hope. After some time, Israel shall "return and seek the Lord their God, and David their king." This will be fulfilled in the latter days (Hosea 3:5). "The Lord their God" and "David their king" refer to the same person, Jesus the Christ. There will be a spiritual and a political restoration to Israel, bringing about the full kingdom of God.

The reference to Jesus as David is one of many among the Old Testament prophets.[4] Thus, Hosea chapter 3 describes, as does chapter 2, Northern Israel's captivity, dispersion, and subsequent restoration. Having proclaimed his punishment, the Lord justifies his actions.

Why Israel Was Rejected

After prophesying of the scattering and gathering of Ephraim, the Lord through Hosea explains the cause of Israel's downfall. In

[4]This work will not treat the full kingdom of God. Suffice it to say that Christ is the David spoken of who will reign politically during the Millennium. For a fuller account, see Bruce R. McConkie, *The Millennial Messiah*, pp. 591–601. Other prophets' references to David include Jeremiah 23:5–6; Ezekiel 34:23; 37:22–28. See also D&C 58:22.

general, the Lord said there was no truth, mercy, or knowledge of God in the land (Hosea 4:1). Specifically, the Lord gives four reasons for their rejection. The first is actually a multitude of reasons but can be summarized as wicked living: swearing, lying, killing, committing adultery. As a result of these conditions, the land would mourn, the people would be taken away, the prophet would fall with them, and the nation (mother) would be destroyed (Hosea 4:2–5).

The second reason for the downfall was a lack of knowledge. The Israelites were not just guilty of illiteracy or lack of intellectual knowledge but rather of a rejection of knowledge given them of the Lord, the law of God. In short, they had sinned against the Lord (Hosea 4:6–7). The priest as well as the people were guilty, resulting in an inability to satisfy their hunger, probably both physically and spiritually. They committed whoredoms, implying the act of procreation, but failing to increase (Hosea 4:8–11).

The third reason for Israel's destruction was their worship of false gods. The description of their worship suggests Baalism along with other types of idol worship. The result of this worship was immorality by their wives and daughters (Hosea 4:12–18). The Lord suggests leniency in his judgment for their spouses and daughters individually because of their environment, but nonetheless the people would fall collectively (Hosea 4:14). Immorality destroys a nation (compare Jacob 3:6). The fourth chapter ends with a warning to Judah not to follow Israel's bad example of harlotry and idolatry (Hosea 4:15–19). Having warned Judah, the Lord returns to his chastisement of Israel or Ephraim.

The Destiny of Ephraim

That Hosea is addressing Ephraim as a nation is evidenced by the many references to her. Seven of the first fourteen verses in chapter 5 refer to Ephraim, and they refer to her nine times. Some of these references are used in negative similitudes, a pattern followed in future chapters that is often very picturesque. The message is primarily a description of Ephraim's wickedness and predicted fall.

Hosea also prophesies that Judah will fall (Hosea 5:5), a seeming contradiction to Hosea 1:7. However, based on historical sequences, the fall of Judah was later; although the text doesn't clarify the time of her fall, it was probably understood by Hosea.

The fifth chapter concludes with the Lord declaring that he will return to his place until Ephraim acknowledges her sins and seeks him (Hosea 5:15). The Lord does not dwell in unholy temples of individuals or nations (Alma 7:21). However, he always extends an invitation for that nation to return to him (Isaiah 55:7; Malachi 3:7).

The sixth chapter begins with Israel saying "Come, and let us return unto the Lord" (Hosea 6:1). The rest of the verse implies that Israel's statement is made after a lengthy period of her being smitten or punished. The following verse gives a time frame for Israel's return: "After two days will he revive us: in the third day he will raise us up, and we shall live in his sight" (Hosea 6:2).

While some look upon this verse as a prophecy of Christ's resurrection, and, of course, all things have their likeness and bear record of him (Moses 6:63), the context suggests that the verse is speaking of the nation of Israel. A day with the Lord is a thousand years with man (Psalm 90:4; 2 Peter 3:8; Abraham 5:13; see also Abraham facs. #2, fig. 1).

Therefore, in the Lord's time, "after two days" equals 2,000 years. "In the third day" could be any part of the next thousand years. Israel was taken away in 721 B.C. It was about 2,550 years from the time of Israel's destruction and scattering until the restoration in 1830, a period of two days and in the third day of the Lord's time.

Furthermore, two thousand years from 721 B.C. would be about the end of the thirteenth century A.D. (1279). This date is approximately the ending of the dark ages and the beginning of the Age of Enlightenment. The Enlightenment is possibly the Lord beginning to revive Israel, but he would not raise her up for part of another day, after the Renaissance and the Reformation. They shall again "live in his sight" (Hosea 6:2).[5] Other Old Testament prophets have foretold these sequential events (Isaiah 28:23–29).

The next verse describes the time when Israel comes to know the Lord (Hosea 6:3). This verse fits the period following the restoration of the Church and encompasses the Church's growth in the knowledge of the Lord.

In the rest of chapter 6, the Lord laments over Israel and Judah's transgressions of the covenant they had made with him. In this lamentation, one of the more well-known verses in Hosea is recorded: "For I desired mercy, and not sacrifice; and the knowledge of God more than burnt offerings" (Hosea 6:6). The Savior quotes it twice during his ministry to refute the self-righteous Pharisees (Matthew 9:13; 12:7). The Lord is more interested in how people relate to each other and come to a knowledge of him than he is in their going through ritual in an attempt to worship him (compare 1 Samuel 15:22–23). This verse also demonstrates that Jehovah, the God of the Old Testament, is a God of mercy as well as justice, something not always understood by readers and teachers of the Old Testament.

Chapters 7 through 10 give many more negative similitudes in describing the downfall of Ephraim. The fall of Judah is also periodically mentioned. A verse-by-verse analysis is not necessary here to understand the main concept of Ephraim being mixed among the Gentiles after she is taken captive (Hosea 8:8).

In the negative similitudes, Ephraim's scattering is compared to a cake not turned (Hosea 7:8). A pancake cooked on only one side is not edible; because Ephraim's wickedness leaves her undesirable to the Lord, she was scattered. Ephraim is compared to "a silly dove without heart: they call to Egypt, they go to Assyria" (Hosea 7:11).

---

[5]In 1843, the Prophet Joseph Smith used Hosea 6:2 as an evidence that the second coming of Christ would not be before the year 1890: "After two days, etc.,—2,520 years" (*TPJS*, p. 286). Unfortunately, his discussion that explained the total years as 2,520 was summarized merely as "etc." Subtracting 2,520 years from 1890 brings one to the year 630 B.C. While this year does not seem to figure into Hosea's lifetime, it is evidence that Joseph considered the prophecy to be fulfilled in the latter days and not as a prophecy of Christ's resurrection. A recording of his explanation would have been very desirable as well as enlightening.

A dove is to return or call to her master, but Ephraim looks elsewhere rather than to the Lord. The Lord will deal with them in their Assyrian conquest. Following other comparisons and descriptions of their wickedness (Hosea chapters 8–10), they are prophesied to be "swallowed up" "among the Gentiles," "wanderers among the nations" (Hosea 8:8; 9:17). Thus, today as people are gathered into the Church or as the remnants of Israel are gathered, we should not be surprised to find patriarchal blessings declaring these people to be of the blood of Ephraim.

Miscellaneous Prophecies

The Lord declares that when Israel was a child (as a nation), he loved him and called him out of Egypt (Hosea 11:1). The house of Israel was in bondage in Egypt until the Lord raised up Moses and called him to lead them back to their land of promise. This, of course, is a similitude of Jesus being in Egypt as a child until the death of Herod (Matthew 2:12–15). The Lord used this prophecy to teach Ephraim that they were not to return to Egypt but were to go into Assyria (Hosea 11:5). At the time of Hosea, Ephraim was seeking an alliance with Egypt. Nonetheless, the Lord promised to gather Ephraim.

Joseph Smith made only one change in the book of Hosea in his translation of the Bible; however, we should not assume that the rest of the book is intact or correct. Actually, the text of Hosea is one of the more corrupt, and Joseph Smith apparently did not have time to work extensively on it (Sperry, p. 278). The change Joseph did make is an important one. It again depicts a message of hope. The Lord's "heart is turned toward [Ephraim], and [his] mercies are extended to gather [her]" (JST, Hosea 11:8). In spite of the people's wickedness, the Lord will not destroy them (Hosea 11:9). He will take them into captivity, scatter them, and later gather them as he has covenanted and as the rest of Hosea testifies. After declaring that Ephraim is not to be totally destroyed, the Lord again affirms that Judah is still faithful at this time (Hosea 11:10–12).

The Lord then returns to the time of his original covenant with Jacob, the father of Israel.

Some have interpreted Hosea 12:3–4 — in which the birth of Jacob, the father of the house of Israel, and his subsequent wrestle with an angel (Genesis 32:24–29) are described — to be a declaration of Jacob's deceptive nature or the beginning of Israel's waywardness. There is another interpretation of this passage. It shows that Jacob was strong from the beginning and prevailed in his mortal probation. However, Jacob's strength will not save his posterity. Each person and each nation will be judged individually (Hosea 12:2). Ephraim as a nation has departed from the Lord, in spite of the Lord's guidance through visions and prophets and his taking Jacob out of the wicked land of Canaan and sending him to Syria to obtain a wife of the covenant (Hosea 12:7–12). The Lord also raised up a prophet to lead Israel out of Egypt, but Ephraim has now provoked the Lord to anger (Hosea 12:13–14).

Hosea 13 declares Ephraim's demise. Ephraim prospered when she followed the Lord but died when she followed Baal. Ephraim is now sinning more and more (Hosea 13:1–2). The Lord is the God who delivered Israel out of Egypt, and there is no savior beside him (Hosea 13:4). Because of Ephraim's sins, she has destroyed herself, and none can help her but the Lord (Hosea 13:9–13). Using the principle of the resurrection as a teaching symbol,[6] the Lord promises to redeem Ephraim from death that is coming upon her (Hosea 13:14). She will be destroyed or die as a nation but will be resurrected or restored. The Lord will destroy her, but he also has the power to take her back up. The Lord concludes the chapter with a declaration of desolation upon Samaria, Ephraim's capital city (Hosea 13:15–16).

---

[6]Hosea 13:14 is similar to 1 Corinthians 15:54–55. Many Bible scholars feel that Paul is quoting or paraphrasing Hosea. While this may be true, another possibility is that both Paul and Hosea are paraphrasing or quoting from an earlier source. The Nephite prophet Abinadi makes reference to the same message and even the same wording as 1 Corinthians 15 in teaching the wicked priests of Noah. He was undoubtedly drawing his information from the plates of brass written before 600 B.C. While the plates probably had Hosea's words on them (see 1 Nephi 5:11–14), the completeness of Abinadi's text suggests another source, and Hosea seems to be drawing upon the principle known, not the text or prophecy.

Conclusion

The last chapter of Hosea ends with an invitation for latter-day Israel to return to the Lord through repentance (Hosea 14:1–3). If Israel will accept the invitation, the Lord promises to heal her of her sins and love her freely (Hosea 14:4). In a positive similitude, the Lord compares latter-day Israel to a lily whose branches shall spread, whose beauty shall be as the olive tree, and whose smell shall be as Lebanon. Those that dwell under this shadow shall be revived (Hosea 14:5–7). That Ephraim is the chief tribe of this return is shown through the response in Hosea 14:8. Ephraim is to acknowledge that she has forsaken her idols, come unto the Lord, and restored his branch.

The prophet Hosea foretold the scattering and gathering of Ephraim, the birthright holder of Israel. While the lily has been planted and the branches have spread much, there is still much growth to come. For those already in the spreading branches or to those who are invited to come and be part of the future growth, the last verse of the book is a fitting conclusion: "Who is wise, and he shall understand these things? prudent, and he shall know them? for the ways of the Lord are right, and the just shall walk in them: but the transgressors shall fall therein" (Hosea 14:9).

Joel—Prophet of the Deliverance in Zion and Judah

Most members of The Church of Jesus Christ of Latter-day Saints are familiar with Joel 2:28–32 because the angel Moroni quoted it to Joseph Smith on the morning of 22 September 1823 as being not yet fulfilled, but it soon would be (JS–H 1:41). However, the rest of the book of Joel is probably not familiar to them. The verses quoted by Moroni are the theme of the book, which is probably why he quoted just those verses. The Lord will pour out his Spirit upon all flesh in preparation for his second coming. The Lord will deliver his people at that time in two major centers, Mount Zion and Jerusalem (see Joel 12:28–32). An analysis of the entire book supports and clarifies this theme.

The superscription (Joel 1:1) has no dating information in it and identifies Joel only as the son of Pethuel. There is no other scriptural clarification of who Joel was, where he was from, or the time of his prophecy. This lack of information has led to much speculation. He has been dated from the eighth century to the fourth century B.C. The later dating (fourth century) is based on the premises of the Assyrians and Chaldeans and the Northern Kingdom of Israel not being mentioned in his text. The text does refer to the dispersion of the Jews (3:2), and the Greeks as slave traders rather than conquerors (3:6). The earlier dating (eighth century) is based on tradition and the chronological sequence of the place of the book in the text. The arguments for later dating do not seem too significant if one accepts a prophet as someone who can see into the future and thus speak of events that have not yet come to pass. The acceptance of either date does not change the message of the book. The message is the important part.

Joel's Intended Audience

The message is given to many generations in the future. Joel begins his text by stating that the events of which he speaks have not happened to this generation nor to previous generations but are to be told to their children and future generations (Joel 1:2–3). In other words, his prophecy will be fulfilled far in the future.

The prophecy that Joel says is to be told to the future generations is a symbolic representation of crops being destroyed by a series of palmerworm insects: the locust, the cankerworm, and the caterpillar (Joel 1:4).

A theory put forth by an eighth century A.D. Jew was that the palmerworm represented Assyria, the locust represented Babylon, the cankerworm represented Macedonia (Greece), and the caterpillar represented Rome. This theory has since been passed on and become a traditional interpretation. Some support is given to the interpretation by the following verses that warn of the drunkenness of the people and a new nation coming upon the land and destroying it (Joel 1:5–7). If Joel lived in the eighth century B.C., this would likely refer to the Assyrian conquest in 721 B.C. and the subsequent conquerings by the succeeding world powers. This seems to be a plausible interpretation, or at least a good application of the verse.[1] Further verification of the above verses being symbolic is given by the Prophet Joseph Smith, who rendered

---

[1]An interpretation, as used here, is what the prophet meant when he uttered the prophecy. An application is the reading of a scripture and applying it to the present-day situation even though the prophet meant something else. Nephi told his readers that he did liken the scriptures unto the Nephites for their profit and learning (1 Nephi 19:23). Jacob refines the process by justifying his application because his people were of the house of Israel (2 Nephi 6:5). These quotations from the Book of Mormon seem to justify the use of applications but suggest that they should be used with some caution.

one of their phrases "whose teeth are *as* the teeth of a lion" (JST, Joel 1:6; italics added – this is one of only three changes the Prophet makes in the book of Joel). Verses 5–7 describe the destruction of a nation, probably the nation of Israel in 721 B.C.

The next several verses of chapter 1 instruct the addressed nation to lament over several negative conditions that are to come upon them because of their wickedness. She is to lament over the husband of her youth (her covenant with Christ), the loss of her sacrifices (ordinances) and priesthood, and the withholding of agricultural blessings to her land (Joel 1:8–13). These conditions would undoubtedly result in the scattering of the nation being addressed (Israel) and the apostasy that followed. The rest of chapter 1 invites the elders and the inhabitants to declare a fast and call a solemn assembly because of the apostasy, since the day of the Lord is at hand (Joel 1:14–20). The elders are to be gathered because there are no blessings of the house of their God. The house of Israel is to gather in preparation for the day of the Lord's judgments, his second coming. Thus, chapter 1 describes the destruction, the apostasy, and the gathering of Israel.

The Gathering to Zion and Jerusalem

The second chapter begins with a warning to Zion that the day of the Lord is nigh at hand (Joel 2:1). According to the teachings of the modern-day prophet Joseph Smith, Zion here has reference to the Americas (*TPJS*, p. 362). The holy mountain is used as Hebrew parallelism to represent the same place.[2] That this does refer to the coming of the Lord being nigh at hand that should cause the inhabitants to tremble in the last days is supported by the fact that Moroni told Joseph Smith that the last verses of Joel 2 would soon be fulfilled (JS–H 1:41).

The succeeding verses of Joel 2 describe the day of the Lord

---

[2]There are different forms of Hebrew parallelism, but the one used here is synonymous parallelism, in which the first phrase is repeated in the second phrase with slightly different wording but giving the same message.

that is to come. The Prophet Joseph Smith cited verse 2 in urging the Saints to prepare for the Second Coming: "It seems to be deeply impressed upon our minds that the Saints ought to lay hold of every door that shall seem to be opened unto them, to obtain foothold on the earth, and be making all the preparation that is within their power for the terrible storms that are now gathering in the heavens, 'a day of clouds, with darkness and gloominess, and of thick darkness,' as spoken of by the Prophet which cannot be now of a long time lingering" (*TPJS*, p. 141).

The day of darkness and gloominess is accompanied by a great and strong people unequaled in previous generations (Joel 2:2–7). These people are probably destroying angels who will come and eliminate the wicked or telestial people. A fire is prophesied to precede them. The fire is probably the glory that attends these angels. Just as God is a consuming fire (Hebrews 2:12–29), the angels appearing in glory will consume the corruptible things of man and beast, as will the Lord's second coming (compare D&C 101:23–24). Further support for their being angels is given in Joel 2:8–9, which states that they cannot be wounded by mortal weapons. This army of the Lord will cause the earth and heaven to quake. The sun and the moon will be darkened, and the stars will not shine. The Lord's voice will precede the army, and his great and terrible day will be ushered in so that the inhabitants of the earth will be unable to abide (Joel 2:10–11). These verses, along with verse 31, are quoted or paraphrased in four sections of the Doctrine and Covenants regarding the Second Coming (D&C 29:14; 34:8–9; 43:18; 84:118).

Returning to the warning to precede this great and terrible day, the people of Zion are invited to turn to the Lord and repent. By doing so, they can escape this terrible evil and receive a blessing that will result in the people offering a sacrifice or oblation in thanksgiving to the Lord (JST, Joel 2:12–14).[3] The trumpet blown

---

[3]See the exact wording in the Bible footnote published by the Church (1979). Joel 2:13–14 are two of the three verses changed by the Prophet Joseph Smith in his translation of the book of Joel. The other one, Joel 1:6, is cited in the body of this chapter.

in Zion will bring about the gathering of the people in preparation for the coming of the bridegroom (Joel 2:15–17). The bridegroom is, of course, Jesus Christ, and the bride is those gathered, or the Church (compare Revelation 19:7–9). The gathering is to take place in two locations—Jerusalem and Zion. The gathering to Jerusalem is described in Joel 2:18–20, and the gathering to Zion is described in Joel 2:21–27.

The gathering to Jerusalem is identified by the designation of the Lord's jealousy for his land and his people (Joel 2:18). In the Book of Mormon, the Savior designated the house of Israel as the Father's people, and the people of Jerusalem as "my people" (3 Nephi 20:29, 46). Apparently the same designation is used here. They are his people because of his earthly lineage. The blessings of prosperity will accompany the Jewish gathering as well as remove their reproach among the heathen (Joel 2:19). The northern army probably represents the Gentiles who will be gathered against Judah in the last days (see Joel 3). The east sea (Dead Sea) and the utmost sea (the Mediterranean), giving the direction of the Gentiles being driven, further identify the subject of this gathering as the Palestine area (Joel 2:20). The Lord will deliver his people.

Shifting the subject to Zion (the American continent), the Lord promises a restoration of the crops that the insects had devoured as recorded in chapter 1. Pastures for the beasts or cattle, along with four of the seven traditional crops raised in Palestine, are enumerated: the fig tree, the vine (grapes), wheat, and oil (olives). These crops will prosper because of the rains sent by the Lord that will cause the people to recognize their Lord and never be ashamed (Joel 2:21–27). From the context of the chapter, this agricultural prosperity describes the settling of America as choice above all other lands (Ether 2:10; 1 Nephi 2:20).

The Spiritual Restoration

After the physical restoration, there will be a spiritual restoration, as the wording of the opening phrase of Joel 2:28 shows: "I will pour out my spirit upon all flesh." The Lord also used the phrase in speaking of the restoration of the endowment upon his apostles (D&C 95:4). The whole of verse 28 and the next three verses were quoted by Moroni as soon to be fulfilled. The spirit poured out upon all flesh as prophesied by Joel has been interpreted to be fulfilled at least in part by the great inventions that have been inspired of God.[4] These inventions have come upon "all flesh," that is, upon everyone living in the land and not just those who are members of the restored church. As Moroni said they were soon to be fulfilled, the majority of these modern conveniences of technology have come in the nineteenth and twentieth centuries, after the restoration of the gospel. The visions and dreams given to the old and the young would include those revelations to prepare people for the Restoration, and those given after the Restoration.[5] The principle of revelation was to continue in the Church as indicated by the ninth Article of Faith. This is equated with the servants and handmaids having the Spirit poured out upon them (Joel 2:29). According to Elder Orson Pratt: "When this prophecy is really fulfilled, all men and women upon the earth will become revelators, receiving from the heavens information and knowledge by the power of that Spirit poured out upon them" (JD 19:169).

The wonders in the heavens and the earth foretold in Joel 2:30–31 were to happen before the Second Coming of the Lord. The terminology used by Joel is common to other scriptures (for example, Matthew 24:39; Isaiah 13:10; D&C 29:14). The specifics of the fulfillment of this prophecy will be better understood at the time they come to pass, as Nephi said concerning the prophecies of Isaiah (2 Nephi 25:7). Joel concludes his soon-to-be fulfilled prophecy with

---

[4]For a more complete analysis of this, see Joseph Fielding Smith, *Doctrines of Salvation*, vol. 1, pp. 172–83.

[5]Many of Joseph Smith's ancestors were given dreams or other types of revelation to prepare them to accept the revelations of their foreordained son and grandson. See Lucy Mack Smith, *History of Joseph Smith by his Mother*, pp. 64–66; B. H. Roberts, CHC 1, chapter 1. These preparatory revelations were not limited to Joseph Smith's family but are cited here merely as an example. Of course, as the Restoration commenced and was added upon, the membership of the Church had great revelations (see HC 1:101). Another example of many, the missionary work of Wilford Woodruff in England is atypical. Matthias F. Cowley, *Wilford Woodruff: History of His Life and Labors*, chapter 23.

the declaration that those who call upon the Lord in these perilous times will be delivered from the terrible destruction. Again, deliverance will take place in the two gathering places — Mount Zion and Jerusalem. The gathering will be initiated and fulfilled through the prophesied remnant of Israel (Isaiah 6:13; 10:20–22; 49:1–6; D&C 133:30–32; Abraham 2:11). The gathering by this remnant was initiated by the visit of the angel Moroni, who announced that God had a work for Joseph Smith to do (JS–H 1:33). After quoting Joel 2:28–32, Joseph Smith commented as follows on his work:

> It is very difficult for us to communicate to the churches all that God has revealed to us, in consequence of tradition; for we are differently situated from any other people that ever existed upon this earth; consequently those former revelations cannot be suited to our conditions; they were given to other people, who were before us; but in the last days, God was to call a remnant, in which was to be deliverance, as well as in Jerusalem and Zion. Now if God should give no more revelations, where will we find Zion and this remnant? The time is near when desolation is to cover the earth, and then God will have a place of deliverance in his remnant, and in Zion.
>
> Take away the Book of Mormon and the revelations, and where is our religion? We have none; for without Zion, and a place of deliverance, we must fall; because the time is near when the sun will be darkened, and the moon turn to blood, and the stars fall from heaven, and the earth reel to and fro. Then, if this is the case, and if we are not sanctified and gathered to the places God has appointed, with all our former professions and our great love for the Bible, we must fall; we cannot stand; we cannot be saved; for God will gather out his Saints from the Gentiles, and then comes desolation and destruction, and none can escape except the pure in heart who are gathered (*TPJS*, pp. 70–71; see also p. 17).

The work has progressed since then and is rapidly spreading throughout the world.

Peter's Quoting of Joel

Many people in the Christian world have neglected to consider the prophecy quoted by Moroni to Joseph Smith as related to the last days. The reason for their misunderstanding is because Peter quoted this prophecy on the day of Pentecost, and they assume it was then fulfilled (Acts 2:16–21). A careful analysis of Peter's words would sustain the fact that he was making an application and not giving an interpretation.[6] Peter is identifying the Spirit that was being poured out upon the Saints gathered at Jerusalem as the same type of Spirit that Joel had prophesied would be poured out in the last days. Peter fully understood that there would be an apostasy for a long time before the Restoration in the last days. On the same occasion that he quoted Joel, he spoke of the times of restitution of all things (Acts 3:19–21). There cannot be a restitution unless something is taken away and then brought back. In his own writings, Peter also shows an awareness of the Apostasy and the Restoration (2 Peter 2:1–4; JST 3:3–13). Furthermore, Peter cuts his quotation of Joel 2:32 short. He does not speak of the two gathering places of salvation but says that only those who call upon the name of the Lord shall be saved (Acts 2:21). Paul also quoted the same shortened version of verse 32 (Romans 10:13). They both seemed to fully understand that Joel was speaking of the time of the Second Coming of the Lord and not the meridian of time. The above interpretation of Peter's quotation is sustained by an address of Elder Orson Pratt in December 1877:

> This prophecy was quoted by the Apostle Peter on the day of Pentecost, when under the influence of the same Spirit. It was not referred to, however, with the intention of declaring its fulfillment at that time, but merely to inform the unbelieving Jews that it was the same Spirit which Joel spoke of. It will be remembered that on the morning of the

---

[6]Some feel that Joel 2:28–32 is a dual prophecy, but I do not believe this can be substantiated. While dual prophecies exist throughout the Old Testament, neither the context of Joel nor Peter supports that thesis.

day of Pentecost, about 120 disciples had received this Spirit. On that occasion, while assembled in the Temple, it operated so powerfully upon them, that the illiterate and unlearned were enabled to speak in different languages, and that it manifested itself in the form of cloven tongues, like fire in appearance. The people who witnessed these operations marveled and wondered exceedingly. But some were inclined to evil, and accused these men of God of drunkenness. It was then that the Apostle Peter, in order to correct any false impression upon the minds of the congregation, arose, and after denying the accusation of these evil-disposed persons, said, "This is that which was spoken by the Prophet Joel," quoting the prophecy nearly word for word.

Some have supposed that the prophecy was then fulfilled. It is very evident to every one who will reflect for a few moments, that such was not the case, but that the Spirit which rested upon those one hundred and twenty was the same Spirit that should, in the last days, be poured out upon all flesh. It is still further evident that it was not then fulfilled, as appears from the following: "I will show wonders in the heavens and in the earth — blood, and fire, and pillars of smoke. The sun shall be turned into darkness, and the moon into blood," etc, having reference to His second coming, when these great events should take place (JD 19:168–69).

The Valley of Decision

Having spoken of the two gathering places in general, Joel returns in chapter 3 to an enlargement upon the prophecies concerning Judah and Jerusalem. As announced, all nations of the Gentiles will be gathered against Judah in the valley of Jehosaphat, where the Lord will plead for his people (Judah) as well as for those of Israel who have been scattered among those Gentile nations (Joel 3:1–2). The valley of Jehosaphat is located outside of Jerusalem and will be the place of the last battle before the long-awaited Messiah comes to rescue his people. The Lord's pleading for his people was also foretold by Isaiah and is used in conjunction with judgment

(Isaiah 3:13–14). Both prophets speak of the injustices that have come upon the Lord's people (Joel 3:3; Isaiah 3:15). Joel speaks of Tyre and Sidon (modern Lebanon) and the coasts of Palestine having mistreated his people and his promise to make recompense upon their heads (Joel 3:4–8). Again the symbolic representation of Tyre and Sidon will be fully understood at some later day, but vengeance is the Lord's and he will repay (Mormon 3:15).

The Lord challenges the Gentiles and the heathens (those who worship other gods) to come to the valley of decision, where he will sit to judge the nations (Joel 3:9–14). At that time, he will show who his people are by his coming to defend them in this great battle. The decision of who is the true Messiah and God of the nations of all the earth will be rendered. While many multitudes will be gathered, they will be no match for the God of the whole earth. Elder Bruce R. McConkie describes the multitudes gathered in the valley of decision as "the hosts of men who must decide whether they will be gathered with the Lord's harvest into his kingdom or be left for the day when the tares and the grain that are not harvested shall be burned.[7]

This battle will be fought just prior to the Lord's coming in glory to the whole world and at the time of the sun, moon, and stars prophecies being fulfilled and causing "the heavens to shake." This shaking is also confirmed in modern revelation, which adds that the shaking is for the Saints' good (D&C 21:6; 35:24; Joel 3:14–16). It will be when the Lord has established his people in his two gathering places of Zion and Jerusalem and is their strength. The roaring out of Zion is the proclaiming of his gospel from the center place of the Church in the Americas, his holy mountain (Joel 3:16–17; compare Isaiah 2:3; 4:2–3). At this time, Jerusalem will also become a holy city as prophesied by Ether, the Jaredite prophet (Ether 13:5, 11). The land of Judah will prosper and all her rivers flow with water. Some of this water will come as a fountain

---

[7]Bruce R. McConkie, *The Mortal Messiah*, Book 1, p. 503. Elder McConkie also gives a very graphic and somewhat detailed description of this final battle and other prophecies of Joel in *The Millennial Messiah*, pp. 454–61.

from under the temple built in Jerusalem (Joel 3:18). There will be other catastrophic events associated with the water coming forth. The Prophet Joseph Smith made this comment about these events:

> Judah must return, Jerusalem must be rebuilt, and the temple, and water come out from under the temple, and the waters of the Dead Sea be healed. It will take some time to rebuild the walls of the city and the temple, &c.; and all this must be done before the Son of Man will make His appearance. There will be wars and rumors of wars, signs in the heavens above and the earth beneath, the sun turned into darkness and the moon to blood, earthquakes in divers places, the seas heaving beyond their bounds; then will appear one grand sign of the Son of Man in heaven. But what will the world do? They will say it is a planet, a comet, etc. But the Son of man will come as the sign of the coming of the Son of Man, which will be as the light of the morning cometh out of the east (*TPJS*, pp. 286–87).

Although great prophecies have been made of Egypt's restoration to the gospel (Isaiah 19), the majority of these people, which includes the Negev of the Sinai (Edom), will not be given their opportunity to have the gospel until after a period of desolation, because of their violence upon Judah and their shedding of innocent blood in their land (Joel 3:19).[8] This may indicate the millennial period in consideration of the dense population of Egypt.

Conclusion

Joel concludes with the Lord's declaration that Judah shall be established forever when these prophecies are fulfilled. This establishment shall come after she has also been cleansed of her sins, which have not as yet been cleansed. The Lord will dwell in Zion, and from this established center he will bring his purposes upon Judah and Jerusalem (Joel 3:20–21).

---

[8]An analysis of Isaiah 19 shows that a savior was to be sent to help Egypt be restored. In 1981, Anwar el Sadat, a leader who did great things for Egypt, was brutally murdered. Perhaps his murder and other similar ones are the innocent blood referred to in Joel 3:20. Isaiah also proclaims a smiting of Egypt in the last days as well as a prophecy of her being healed.

While the book of Joel contains only three chapters and totals about four and one-half pages, the message is relevant to our day. Much of the restoration to Israel and Judah that is there foretold has come to pass, but there remains much more that will also soon come about.

Amos — The House of Israel among All Nations

The superscription of the book of Amos (Amos 1:1) dates his prophecy in the days of Uzziah or Azariah king of Judah (2 Kings 15:1–2) and Jeroboam king of Israel (2 Kings 14:23–24). Uzziah began his reign in the twenty-seventh year of Jeroboam's reign, and Jeroboam reigned for forty-one years. The most probable date of the beginning of Uzziah's reign is about 791 B.C. He ruled for about fifteen years while Jeroboam was still king; therefore the date of the prophecy is between about 791 and 777 B.C. The superscription also dates the prophecy as two years before the earthquake.

There is no account of the earthquake in the historical books of Kings or Chronicles. The prophet Zechariah does refer to this catastrophic event in the days of Uzziah (Zechariah 14:5) but gives no more specific date. Therefore, Amos can only be dated somewhere within the fifteen-year period between 791 and 777 B.C. The book is traditionally placed third in the canon of the Twelve Prophets, implying that he followed Hosea and Joel but preceded Obadiah, Jonah, and Micah. Although this placement is chronologically controversial, the superscriptions of Hosea and Micah support this theory. Following this reasoning, Amos would have preceded the prophet Isaiah by some thirty-five to fifty years.

It is also possible that Amos gave more prophecies than the one recorded in the Bible. Chapters 1 through 7 seem to be a continuous prophecy given to Northern Israel in Jeroboam's day. Chapters 8 and 9 may have been given on another occasion, or they may be a continuation of the same prophecy. Amos's mission was to warn of Northern Israel's coming downfall if they did not repent. His message was that although Israel was to be destroyed, it would not be utterly destroyed but would be sifted or scattered among all the nations of the earth (Amos 9:8–9). All aspects of his written text relate to that central theme.

The Law of Retaliation

One of the most unusual approaches of the Old Testament prophets is used by Amos. Upon entering the city of Bethel (Amos 7:10), the site of their temple, he announced that "the Lord will roar from Zion, and utter his voice from Jerusalem," causing the land of Israel to suffer (Amos 1:2). He then began a scathing pronouncement of the Lord's judgments forthcoming upon the seven nations surrounding Israel (Amos 1:3–2:5). The first three nations were Gentile nations: Syria, of which Damascus was the capital; Gaza, the nation of the Philistines; and Tyrus, the nation of the Phoenicians. The next three nations were the blood relatives of Israel: Edom, the descendants of Esau, brother of Jacob (Genesis 36); and Ammon and Moab, the descendants of Lot and his two daughters (Genesis 19). The seventh nation rebuked was Israel's counterpart, Judah. These chastisements were undoubtedly pleasing to the people and leaders of Israel.

The reasons for the rebukes can readily be found in the text (Amos 1:3–2:5). And an important principle of the gospel is confirmed in Amos's pronouncements. Each nation is informed that the Lord's judgment is coming upon them "for three transgressions . . . and for four." In 1833, the Lord revealed the "law of retaliation" and the "law of war" to the Prophet Joseph Smith regarding the persecution that had come upon the Saints in Missouri. The essence of these laws was that individuals or nations were to lift up a standard of peace three times to those who offended them. If their enemy came upon them the fourth time after having been warned, the Lord would deliver the enemy into their hands, and the Lord himself would fight their battles for them. These laws, the Lord proclaimed, he had given to his ancient prophets (D&C 98:23–38). Each of the seven surrounding nations had sinned against the Lord three times and a fourth. The Lord was therefore bringing his judgments upon them. Thus Amos verifies what the Lord revealed in the Doctrine and Covenants.

Israel's Transgressions

Having gotten Israel's attention, Amos turns to the sins of which they were guilty that were to bring the Lord's judgments upon them. Israel also had four transgressions against them. Israel's first sin enumerated by Amos was the selling of the poor people into slavery. In Amos's words, "They sold the righteous for silver, and the poor for a pair of shoes" (Amos 2:6). Not only was Israel neglecting the poor, but they were also using them and the righteous to further their own financial gain.

Israel's second sin was one of immorality. However, it was immorality carried on in the name of religion, of which Israel had been repeatedly warned. The pagan worship of Baal included the practice of temple prostitution. Israel, who knew better, was profaning the name of Jehovah by a man and his father going in to the same maid under the guise of religion (Amos 2:7).

The third sin of Israel was a failure to care for the poor among them (Amos 2:8). The Lord places a high priority on the care of the poor (Alma 34:28; D&C 104:18). Under the law, a person's outer clothing could be taken as a pledge for indebtedness, but it was to be returned to the person by evening because it was used as a cover for sleeping. The rich oppressors were failing to return these pledges and were using the pledged garments for their own comfort and satisfaction.

The fourth sin of Israel was one of failing to keep their covenants. The Lord, through Amos, reminded Israel that he had destroyed the Amorites out of this land and brought Israel out of Egypt to occupy it. The Lord had intended that Israel's sons be prophets and enter covenants to be Nazarites, who pledged to abstain from wine and other things. However, their fathers were encouraging these young sons to drink wine and discouraging them from honoring their priesthood or becoming prophets (Amos 2:9–12). This is the equivalent of encouraging the breaking of the Word of Wisdom and discouraging young men to go on missions in our day.

Because of these four sins, the Lord proclaims that the nation shall fall. Their flight shall fail them; their strength shall fail them; their armies shall not be able to defend the nation; and those who are swift of foot or even ride horses shall not be delivered from the enemy. Even the most courageous will be driven before the onslaught of the invading army (Amos 2:13–16). This army is undoubtedly the Assyrian conquest in 721 B.C.

The Covenant with Israel

Amos relayed the Lord's overall complaint against Israel. The Lord reminded them that Israel was the only family of all the families of the earth with whom he had made a covenant (Amos 3:2). However, a covenant involves two people, and the Lord asks Israel, "Can two walk together unless they are agreed?" (Amos 3:3). The Lord then asks several other questions concerning things that are obvious (Amos 3:4–6). Turning some of those questions into statements, the Lord says that the roaring of a lion is evidence that he has found a prey; the blowing of a trumpet (of warning) in a city makes people afraid; and, finally, when there is evil in a city, the Lord knows it (JST, Amos 3:6). The Lord then puts forth one of his rules of action: "Surely the Lord God will do nothing *until* he revealeth the secret unto his servants the prophets" (JST, Amos 3:7; italics added).[1] The Lord then declares that the lion has roared and the Lord has prophesied (Amos 3:8). The lion probably represents the nation of Assyria, who would come upon the prey,

---

[1]These are the first of nine variant verses in the Joseph Smith Translation of the book of Amos. The other seven are: 4:3; 5–6; 6:10; 7:3, 6; and 9:8. These two changes and the two in chapter 7 are the significant ones and thus the only ones footnoted in the 1979 edition of the Bible published by the Church.

the nation of Israel. The nation of Northern Israel is warned by the Lord's servants, the prophets, that she is facing a judgment upon her.

One of the better known Old Testament scriptures to Latter-day Saints is Amos 3:7. It has been quoted repeatedly by modern-day prophets. Joseph Smith called Amos 3:7 "the grand rule of heaven . . . that nothing should ever be done on earth without revealing the secret to his servants the prophets" (*TPJS*, p. 265). He also quoted it as evidence that the sign of the Son of Man had not been given because the Lord had not shown the sign to him, the prophet (*TPJS*, p. 280).

Various other General Authorities have quoted Amos 3:7 to show the necessity of a prophet in these latter days. Elder LeGrand Richards stated: "No one can look for a work here upon this earth that isn't headed by a prophet. The Lord has never done a work that he has recognized without a prophet at its head."[2] Elder Mark E. Petersen taught, "When there are no prophets, there is no divine direction, and without such direction the people walk in darkness. It is an infallible sign of the true church that it has in it divinely chosen, living prophets to guide them, men who receive current revelation from God and whose recorded work becomes new scripture."[3] He also testified of Joseph Smith through quoting Revelation 14:6–7, the prophecy of another angel restoring the everlasting gospel, and Amos 3:7, and reasoning:

> Then what would God do about the angel bringing the gospel back to earth in modern times? There were no prophets on earth to whom he could come. The world no longer even believed in them. If the Lord would do nothing—not even send his angel to earth to restore the gospel—without the services of a living prophet, how could He accomplish his divine purpose? How could the angelic visitation predicted for the latter days be consummated if there were no prophets to receive it.

---

[2]CR, October 1975, p. 75.
[3]CR, April 1978, p. 95.

God could only do one thing, and that was to raise up a new prophet for this particular purpose, and this he did in the person of Joseph Smith Jr., who lived near Palmyra, New York, in 1823. It was this young man to whom the angel Moroni came.[4]

In the text of Amos, the Lord invites the neighboring countries of Egypt and Ashdad (Philistia) to observe the great tumults and oppression in the land of Israel (Amos 3:9–10). Because of these conditions, an adversary is going to destroy their strength and palaces. The coming destruction is compared to the shepherd who takes two legs or the piece of an ear (Israel and Syria) out of the mouth of a lion (Assyria)[5] (Amos 3:11–12). The Lord is saying that there will be a remnant of Israel saved; they will not all be destroyed. While a remnant will be saved, the sacred altar of Bethel where both Abraham and Jacob had great visions will be destroyed (Genesis 12:8; 28:10–22). The horns of the altar were a protection to those who innocently took someone's life (1 Kings 1:50). Since Israel was not innocently sinning, the horns would be cut off and not be a place of refuge (Amos 3:14). The rich palaces that were built through violence and robbing of the poor were also to come to an end (Amos 3:15). The Lord had warned them through the prophet Amos.

Amos addresses the kine (women) of Bashan as the instigators of the poor being oppressed. Their rich social customs and habits are supported by the encouragement they give to their husbands. The day will come when the Lord will take "every *one* before *his enemy,* and ye shall *be* cast *out of your palaces*" (JST, Amos 4:1–3; italics added). The hypocrisy of Israel is proclaimed in their transgressions at the same time as they make sacrifices and offerings (Amos 4:4–5).

The Lord has tried repeatedly to bring Israel to repentance through the elements. These include famine, the withholding of

---

[4]CR, October 1983, p. 43.

[5]Northern Israel and Syria are confederates at this time and will threaten to come against Judah (Isaiah 7:1–2). Since the tribes of Reuben and Gad and half the tribe of Manasseh lived on the east side of the Jordan River, this may also be a reference to that territory.

rain, no drinking water, and mildew. They had also experienced war and destruction, but to no avail. Therefore, their destruction was imminent, and they were invited to meet their God (Amos 4:6–13).

The destruction was not to be total. A tenth of the fallen virgin, she who has been immoral with other gods, would remain (Amos 5:1–3). This could have reference to the number who would be taken into Assyria as captives or to the number who would be left behind to intermarry with the men from Babylon and other nations whom the Assyrians brought in after they conquered Israel (2 Kings 17:24).[6] The latter seems the more probable because of the verses that follow. Those of the house of Israel are invited to seek the Lord and live. They are further warned to avoid various areas of the country that will not escape the captivity (Amos 5:4–5). The next several verses repeat the invitation to seek the Lord and also describe him, his past accomplishments, the people's sins, and the conditions for the remnant of Joseph to receive the graciousness of the Lord (Amos 5:6–15). The coming destruction is announced as a day of darkness (Amos 5:16–20). While the wording may suggest the day of the Lord to be the Second Coming, the context does not support such an interpretation. If it is a Second Coming prophecy, it has to be in the form of a dual prophecy, the Second Coming being after the pattern of the coming destruction upon Northern Israel.

The Lord now turns to his distaste for the hypocritical rituals of sacrifice that the people have apparently been performing and the captivity that is to come (Amos 5:21–27). A warning to those who are at ease in Zion follows. Their ease comes from trust in the greatness of their nation (Amos 6:1–2). The Zion spoken of here must refer to the false concept of a Zion people, not the geographical location, because it fits neither the city of Zion on Mt. Moriah in Jerusalem nor the definition of North and South America given by

---

[6]The intermarriage of the Babylonians and others with the remnant of Northern Israel that remained is in fulfillment of the allegory of the house of Israel prophesied by Zenos and recorded in the Book of Mormon. This intermarriage would represent the wild olive branch (Gentiles) being grafted into Israel or the tame olive tree (Jacob 5:7–10).

the Prophet Joseph Smith (*TPJS*, p. 362). To show the disparity of their being at ease, the Lord cites the fall of other surrounding nations (Amos 6:2). Their trust in the mountain of Samaria identifies them as the people of Northern Israel. A description of their casual living and lack of concern for the welfare of the people of Joseph is part of this final warning of this section of the book (Amos 6:3–6). Again the Lord declares their coming captivity and the completeness of the destruction (Amos 6:7–14).

The Visions of Amos

In what appears to be another section of the book, perhaps given at a different time, Amos relates three visions he has seen. All three visions have the same message — the coming destruction — and two of the three have the same conclusion.

The first vision is of grasshoppers destroying the grass of the land. In response to Amos's plea for mercy so that the promises previously extended to Jacob or the house of Israel could be fulfilled, "the Lord said, concerning Jacob, Jacob shall repent for this, therefore I will not utterly destroy him" (JST, Amos 7:1–3). The second vision is of a destruction by fire with a similar plea by Amos and an almost identical response from the Lord — Jacob will not be utterly destroyed (JST, Amos 7:4–6). The original wording of the KJV in both verses 3 and 6, "The Lord repented of this," exemplifies a false principle that has been added to the original text and thus shows the need for the JST. The Lord's nature is one of total righteousness (Helaman 13:38); he does not need to repent.

The third vision shown to Jacob is of the Lord standing on a wall with a "plumbline" in his hand. The Lord told Amos that he would set a "plumbline" in the midst of his people Israel and would not pass by them more. Their places of worship and sanctuaries would be destroyed, and the house of Jeroboam would have the sword come against it (Amos 7:7–9). A plumb line is a device used to square a wall or a building. The Lord is therefore declaring that Israel is out of alignment, and he will no longer ignore it but will correct its defectiveness. The correction will include the removal of Jeroboam the king, a major cause of Israel's being out of line.

The Call of Amos

The last of the three visions of Amos that he related to the people, and perhaps all three, caused Amaziah, the priest of Bethel, to send word to King Jeroboam that Amos was conspiring against him and creating problems in the midst of Israel. Amaziah then directed Amos to flee to Judah and prophesy, but to not prophesy to Bethel anymore (Amos 7:10–13). Amos's response to Amaziah's rebuke gives us information about Amos's call to be a prophet.

Amos declared that he was not a prophet or the son of a prophet but was a herdsman and a picker of "sycomore" fruit,[7] and that the Lord called him to go to Israel and to prophesy to the Lord's covenant people (Amos 7:14–15). That Amos was not a prophet is telling the reader that he was not called as such prior to this calling. Furthermore, he was not in line to become a prophet because of his lineage or heredity. He was a common, everyday herdsman and fruit laborer when the call came to him. Here is a lesson to the world and a confirmation to the members of the Church today. The Lord does not have a professional clergy but calls people from ordinary walks of life to fulfill his ministerial needs.

Having defended his calling, Amos refuted Amaziah by further prophesying against Amaziah the priest. He pronounced that Amaziah's wife will become a harlot in the city, his sons and daughters will fall by the sword, his land will be divided, and he himself will go into captivity in a polluted land, the land of Israel's captor (Amos 7:16–17). Such was the prophesied fate of him who raised his hand against the Lord's anointed.

Amos Again Prophesies

The last two chapters of Amos are four prophecies given without any historical setting. Two of these prophecies are prophecies of

---

[7]Sycomore fruit is a fig that has been pierced to make it ripen.

doom, containing messages of Israel's downfall. The other two are prophecies of hope, things that will bring some blessings to them. The first of each type of prophecy is in the form of a vision, and the second is apparently associated with the vision.

The first vision is a basket of summer fruit. The interpretation of the fruit basket is that the end had come upon the people of the nation of Israel (Amos 8:1–3). The summer fruit indicates that the harvest is over, the fruit has been picked, and the season is ended. Israel's destruction is once more announced. The causes for the destruction are then enumerated. The primary reason seems to be the neglect and the subjugation of the poor. The many ways that this is done include making the ephah small (inaccurate measures), the shekel great (overcharging), and falsifying balances (weights). None of these dishonest acts will be forgotten by the Lord (Amos 8:1–7). Because of such practices, the land will tremble, the earth will be darkened, and mourning will be prevalent (Amos 8:8–10).

Following this vision, Amos records a prophecy of the future. The Lord designates a famine in the days to come. This famine is not one "of bread, nor a thirst for water but of hearing the words of the Lord." Amos further prophesies that people will "wander from sea to sea, and from the north even to the east" seeking the word of the Lord but being unable to find it (Amos 8:11–12). To Latter-day Saints, this is clearly a description of the apostasy, that period when the gospel became perverted and the authority to administer the ordinances of salvation was taken from the earth. Those in this time, as in other times, who follow false gods as did the people in Dan and Beersheba "shall fall, never to rise again" (Amos 8:14). There is no way to raise them from their fall in this life because there is no source of help. Of course there will be a full opportunity for all in the spirit world following their mortal deaths.[8]

The above prophecy of Amos (8:11–12) has oft been quoted by the General Authorities, either to announce the end of the

---

[8]For verification of an opportunity to hear the gospel being provided for those who had not had an opportunity in this life, see 1 Peter 3:18–20; 4:5–6; and D&C 138:25–32.

spiritual drought through the restoration of the gospel,[9] or to show how aptly it describes the people and the conditions of today.[10]

The third prophecy of the last section of the book is another vision shown to Amos. He sees the Lord standing upon an altar and smiting the inhabitants of the land. He proclaims that wherever the people go, they will not be able to escape the wrath that the Lord is sending upon them (Amos 9:1–4).

After rehearsing a few of the things he has done in the earth (Amos 9:5–7), the Lord pronounces one of the great prophecies of the book of Amos and of the whole Old Testament and the theme of the entire book. He declares that his eyes are upon the sinful kingdom of Northern Israel and that it will be destroyed from off the face of the earth. Although the nation will be removed, the people will not all be eliminated. As previously prophesied (JST, Amos 7:3, 6), the house of Jacob was not to be utterly destroyed. They were, however, to be sifted among all nations, as corn (grain) is sifted in a sieve, but every kernel of that corn will be accounted for by the Lord, who knows all things (Amos 9:8–9).

President Spencer W. Kimball quoted this passage with a slightly modified ending that verified this interpretation. Said he: "Yet the Lord has not forgotten Israel, for though Israel was to be sifted among all nations, the Lord nevertheless said, 'Yet shall not the least grain fall upon the earth' and be lost" (Amos 9:9).[11] Just as one sparrow shall not fall to the ground without the knowledge of God (Matthew 10:29–31), the house of Israel, who were numbered in the days of the separation of the sons of Adam (Deuteronomy 32:8), are of more value to the Father than a sparrow.

His program of scattering Israel among all the nations of the earth was for two purposes: for the benefit of Israel, and for the benefit of all the nations among whom they were to be scattered.

---

[9]See Spencer W. Kimball, CR, April 1964, pp. 93–94.

[10]See Joseph B. Wirthlin, CR, October 1975, p. 155. This is only one of many such pronouncements.

[11]Kimball, Spencer W., *Ensign*, December 1975, p. 4.

In their wickedness, the children of Israel needed to be separated from each other and purged of their iniquities through living among other peoples. While the other people did not have the gospel in its fulness, they did possess teachings of moral value to help make Israel a more honorable people. As subsequent generations came into the world, the time or times would come when the gospel would be preached again upon the earth, and those of the house of Israel who lived among the Gentiles would be able to accept the gospel and become a part of fulfilling the covenant made to Abraham, Isaac, and Jacob. Those who were valiant in their premortal life would recognize the message of the gospel on earth because it is a part of their previous beliefs. As Jesus said in his mortal ministry, "My sheep hear my voice and I know them, and they follow me" (John 10:27; compare D&C 29:7).

As a restoration takes place, those to whom the keys and authority are given are commissioned to teach the gospel to those around them. As they go among the various nations of the earth, those of the blood of Israel are gathered. Those who are not of the blood of Israel are given the opportunity to come in and be adopted or numbered with Israel (3 Nephi 30:1–2). Through this procedure, the covenant made to Abraham is fulfilled—that through him would "all families of the earth be blessed" (Genesis 12:3; Abraham 2:9–10). Thus the scattering of the ten tribes in the days of Amos was a blessing to all peoples of the earth, as eventually all nations will have the gospel preached to them to gather out Israel and give the other inhabitants an opportunity to be part of the covenant people.

It is often assumed that those who are members of the Church today have been adopted into the house of Israel. This is not a correct assumption. The majority of the members, whether born into the Church or converted, are literal descendants of Jacob. This is confirmed by revelation, patriarchal blessings, and modern-day prophets (D&C 86:8–10; 113:17).[12] The Lord has also declared that

---

[12]For a more complete analysis of the members of the Church being literal descendants of Abraham and Israel, see Monte S. Nyman, "A Second Gathering of Israel," in *Doctrines for Exaltation* (Salt Lake City: Deseret Book Company, 1989).

few Gentiles would join the Church in spite of the opportunity to do so (D&C 45:28–29; Isaiah 41:11–12; *TPJS*, p. 15). Therefore, we are living today in the age of the gathering together of the house of Israel from among all the nations of the earth.

The last prophecy recorded in Amos is concerning the eventual result of the gathering out of the house of Israel from among the nations. In the day of the gathering, the Lord will "raise up the tabernacle of David that is fallen . . . and . . . build it as in the days of old" (Amos 9:11). This has reference to the establishment of the full kingdom of God among the original twelve tribes of Jacob. The twelve tribes will be reunited with one king ruling over them all. That king will be Christ, "THE LORD OUR RIGHTEOUSNESS" (Jeremiah 23:5–6). He will be the descendant of David, who was promised that his seed would reign forever, or eternally (2 Samuel 7:16).[13] He is the "KING OF KINGS, AND LORD OF LORDS" (Revelation 19:16).

The kingdom will engulf the Edomites, descendants of Esau the brother of Jacob, and the heathen nations who will be called by the name of the Lord (Amos 9:12). The earth will continually bear crops for the benefit of the people (Amos 9:13). Amos concludes with the declaration that Israel will come out of captivity and build and inhabit the waste cities. They will be prosperous agriculturally and be permanently established in their land of promise (Amos 9:14–15). The covenant to Abraham, Isaac, Jacob or Israel, Joseph, Judah, and Ephraim will be fulfilled.

Conclusion

The southern herdsman from Tekoa, the little town outside of Jerusalem, fulfilled a successful mission to the neighboring sister Israelite country to the north. In spite of political pressure, he fearlessly delivered the message the Lord sent him to proclaim. The

---

[13]See also *TPJS*, p. 339. This has been interpreted by Elder Bruce R. McConkie as Jesus Christ. See *The Promised Messiah*, pp. 191–95.

fall of Israel was soon to come, but the Lord showed him the glorious future of Israel as well. She would not be utterly destroyed but would be scattered among all the nations of the earth. In the last days her people were to again be gathered. Today we are living in the day of which he prophesied.

The Vision of Obadiah Concerning Edom

The book of Obadiah is the smallest book of the prophets and also the smallest book in the Old Testament. The superscription, now incorporated in verse 1, calls the book "the vision of Obadiah. Thus saith the Lord God concerning Edom."

Edom is the homeland of Esau's posterity that dwelt in Mount Seir (Genesis 36:1, 8). Esau is the son of Isaac and the twin brother of Jacob. The Lord told their mother, Rebekah, "Two nations are in thy womb" (Genesis 25:23).

Why do we know so little of the nation of Esau and so much about Jacob or Israel? Notwithstanding the fact that Jacob sired the covenant people, the chosen people, there is seemingly more said about every other "noncovenant" nation than there is about Esau (Edom). The prophecy of Obadiah is thus somewhat unusual.

Another point of conjecture and curiosity are the pointed references in Obadiah to such terms as *Mount Zion, saviors, house of Jacob and Joseph,* and others, which have become common expressions in the Church. Nearly all of the world's scholars completely avoid the questions and use many words to say very little. However, an analysis of the whole book shows that these phrases are the essence of the book's message. The nation of Esau will be blessed through those of the house of Joseph, who will thus become their saviors.

61

Esau-Edom

Basic to any investigation of the book of Obadiah is a brief review of Esau as the originator of the nation of Edom, upon which Obadiah appears to call down the wrath of God.

Esau can be interpreted as "actor or agent." The Bible also suggests that the name means "red and covered with hair" (Genesis 25:25), and further implies a connection with the name "Edom" coming from the "red pottage" Esau asked of Jacob (Genesis 25:30).

The history of this people — neighbors of the Israelites on the east and south — is very vague. As a typical commentary states:, "All the monuments and written records of the Edomites have perished, so what information we have concerning them comes from the writings of their neighbors and enemies — the Israelites, Egyptians, Assyrians and Babylonians — and from archaeological exploration."[1]

Obadiah

Another foundation stone for understanding the book of Obadiah is knowledge of the author. *Obadiah* is a fairly common name in the Bible. There are over twelve references to an Obadiah, in addition to the author of the short prophecy that bears the name of Obadiah. Some of these references are:

1. Author of the prophecy that bears the name of Obadiah.
2. The governor of Ahab's house, described as a man who feared Jehovah greatly (1 Kings 18:3).
3. A son of Azel, of the family of Saul (1 Chronicles 8:38).
4. A son of Izrahiah of Issachar (1 Chronicles 7:3).
5. A Gadite who joined David at Ziklag (1 Chronicles 12:9).
6. The father of Ishmaiah (1 Chronicles 27:19).
7. A son of Hananiah and grandson of Zerubbabel (1 Chronicles 3:21).
8. A Merarite Levite (2 Chronicles 34:12).
9. A son of Shemaiah of Jeduthun (1 Chronicles 9:16 but in Nehemiah 11:17 Abda).

---

[1] Buttrick, *The Interpreter's Dictionary of the Bible.*

The Vision of Obadiah Concerning Edom

10. An officer of Jehoshaphat (2 Chronicles 17:7).
11. A son of Jehiel (Ezra 8:9).
12. One who sealed the covenant with Nehemiah (Nehemiah 10:5).
13. The head of a family of doorkeepers (Nehemiah 12:25).
14. A Levite overseer of the temple repairs in the time of King Josiah of Judah (2 Chronicles 34:12).[2]

The name Obadiah means "a servant or worshiper of Jehovah." Whether the author of the prophecy is connected with any of the other Obadiahs is not known. Such a connection would possibly shed light on the message as well as the dating of the book.

Book of Obadiah

Obadiah is the fourth of the twelve minor prophets according to the Hebrew Bible and fifth according to the Greek. Most writers classify him as living in the eighth century according to chronological arrangement, although there are great differences of opinion on this particular point. The dates usually fall into three possible periods: 872–700 B.C.; 620–585 B.C.; or 380–312 B.C. "The ancient Jews believed the author of the book of Obadiah was the governor in the house of Ahab."[3] This would favor the earlier period. There is also something to be said about a chronological order being followed in the Twelve Prophets that would favor this early date.

There are many citations that indicate several marked similarities between Obadiah and Jeremiah. Such similarities may suggest the second date mentioned above:

Obadiah	Jeremiah
verses 1–4	49:14–16
verse 6	49:9–10
verse 8	49:7

---

[2]*Funk and Wagnall Dictionary.*

[3]John Kitton, ed., *The Cyclopaedia of Biblical Literature*, 10th edition, 2 volumes (New York: Ivison & Newman & Co., 1853).

63

Much controversy has raged over these resemblances, with three possible solutions being offered: (1) Jeremiah copied from Obadiah; (2) Obadiah copied from Jeremiah; (3) both copied from another original source. A fourth possible solution would be that the Lord revealed the same information to both of them.

There are also some prophecies in Amos 1:11, Jeremiah 49:22, Ezekiel 25:12–14, and Psalm 137:7, which are similar to Obadiah's prophecies against Edom. These prophecies may help in the interpretation of the book. One might also compare D&C 1:36.

The Book's Message

The prophecy of Obadiah may be divided into four convenient parts:

1. Announcement of doom or destruction for Edom (vv. 1–9).
2. The reasons for this indictment (vv. 10–14).
3. The judgments of God and retribution among the nations (vv. 15–16).
4. The restoration and exaltation of Israel and the coming of the Saviour on Mount Zion (vv. 17–21).

The Doom of Edom

The first nine verses prophesy of Edom's downfall and are undoubtedly dual prophecies. They refer to the days of Obadiah and to the destruction of the wicked in the latter days. In the preface to the Doctrine and Covenants, the Lord equates his judgment upon the wicked as being upon Idumea, or the world (D&C 1:36). Idumea is another designation of the geographical area of Edom. The ambassador sent among the heathen (Obadiah 1:1) could be those heathens or non-Israelite nations who have looked down upon the nation of the Edomites and verbally and physically brought her down. In the dual aspect of the latter days, it could be the prophets and missionaries who have taught the gospel to the Gentiles and destroyed the wicked of the world through conversion. These converts have thus despised the world's philosophy (Obadiah 1:2; compare Isaiah 13:1–5). Teman was once known for its worldly philosophy (see Job 2:11; 4), but lost this designation, as will also happen to the wisdom of the world at the time of the destruction of the wicked (Obadiah 1:8–9).

The Reasons for Destruction

In verses 10 through 14, the Lord reveals three reasons for Edom's destruction: (1) violence against Jacob, (2) spoiling the cities of Israel when opportunity came, and (3) delivering those of Israel who escaped from their oppressors back into their hands. According to Obadiah's vision, since the days of Jacob and Esau, the Edomites have not only warred against the covenant people of Jacob but have also rejoiced when Gentile countries have conquered and scattered them (Obadiah 1:10–12). Following the various defeats of the Israelites by other nations, the Edomites were quick to enter those fallen cities and take hold of the Israelites' possessions for their own (Obadiah 1:13). Last of all, in the various conquests of Jacob's children, the people of Esau, probably being very familiar with escape routes, were quick to block the escape of any who had survived the destruction and return them to the conquering armies (Obadiah 1:14). For these reasons, Edom was going to experience similar things at the hands of their enemies.

Retribution among the Nations

In an apparent projection into the destruction of the world in the last days or in "the day of the Lord," Edom, the wickedness of the world, was going to have the same things happen to her that she had seen and had helped promulgate upon Israel (Obadiah 1:15). The conquest of Edom would come from all the nations of the heathens or the Gentiles (v. 16). The Lord again teaches a concept found in the Book of Mormon that "the judgments of God will overtake the wicked; and it is by the wicked that the wicked are punished; for it is the wicked who stir up the hearts of the children of men unto bloodshed" (Mormon 4:5). This will not totally destroy Edom, for that will be done at the second coming of the Lord, "the end of the world or the destruction of the wicked, which is the end of the [telestial] world" (JS–M 1:4).

The Restoration upon Mount Zion

Having pronounced this terrible message of doom, the Lord, through Obadiah, now turns, in a typical fashion revealed to other prophets, to a message of hope. While Edom and its symbolic representation, the world, will be destroyed, those who respond to the message of the Restoration can be saved. This salvation opportunity will come from Mount Zion, which are the Americas as defined by the Prophet Joseph Smith: "The whole of America is Zion itself from north to south, and is described by the Prophets, who declare that it is the Zion where the mountain of the Lord should be, and that it should be in the center of the land" (*TPJS*, p. 362). Through the deliverance furnished upon Mount Zion, Israel will again possess their promised lands, the Americas will be given to Joseph (3 Nephi 15:12–13), and Jerusalem or Palestine will be given to Judah and other tribes of Israel (Obadiah 1:17).

Obadiah describes the house of Jacob as a fire and the house of Joseph as a flame, with the house of Esau being as stubble (Obadiah 1:18). The house of Jacob through the tribe of Joseph will consume the nation of Esau as fire destroys a field of grain stubble. This unusual analogy probably refers to the absorption of the house of Esau into the house of Israel by means of the ambassadors sent among them to teach the gospel, as mentioned in verse 1. This interpretation is consistent with Isaiah's prophecy of Babylon's destruction in a similar way. Spiritual Babylon, representing the wickedness of the world (D&C 1:14), will be destroyed by lifting up an ensign (the Book of Mormon) and by a great people in the mountains (Saints) combining with the Lord's hosts (angels) coming from heaven[4] (Isaiah 13:1–5). Those who are not converted will be

---

[4]See also Moses 7:52. The Prophet Joseph asked "how righteousness and truth are going to sweep the earth as with a flood." He answered, "Men and angels are to be co-workers in bringing to pass this great work" (*TPJS*, p. 84). President Ezra Taft Benson has urged a massive flooding of the earth with the Book of Mormon (CR, October 1988, p. 4).

destroyed at Christ's second coming. Although Obadiah doesn't mention this phase as does the Isaiah prophecy, it is implied in the rest of verse 18: "There shall not be any remaining of the house of Esau." Verses 19 and 20 discuss the house of Israel possessing various surrounding nations. What happens to Edom as a nation will happen to all other nations of the heathen or gentiles. When it is remembered that father Abraham was given all of these lands, it is logical that this occupation describes the fulfillment of the covenant made with Abraham. Those who are destroyed and didn't hear the gospel will have such an opportunity elsewhere.

Saviors on Mount Zion

One of the well-known phrases among Latter-day Saints is taken from the last verse of Obadiah—"saviors upon mount Zion." The term was used by the Prophet Joseph Smith, which accounts for its use among members of the Church today. Although most Church members could not justify its use in the context of Obadiah, Joseph did give a valid interpretation. First of all, let us examine Joseph Smith's statements.

In May 1841, Joseph spoke on the subject of election in the flesh of Abraham's seed. In relation to this subject he said, "The election of the promised seed still continues, and in the last day, they shall have the Priesthood restored unto them, and they shall be the 'saviors on Mount Zion,' the ministers of our God; if it were not for the remnant which was left, then might men now be as Sodom and Gomorrah" (*TPJS*, p. 189).

In October 1841, Joseph "presented baptism for the dead as the only way that man can appear as saviors on Mount Zion" (*TPJS*, p. 191). In April 1842, as he preached on the subject of baptism for the dead, he declared: "We are commanded to be baptized for our dead, thus fulfilling the words of Obadiah, when speaking of the glory of the latter-day: And saviors shall come upon Mount Zion to judge the remnant of Esau, and the kingdom shall be the Lord's" (*TPJS*, p. 223).

In January 1844, the Prophet gave a discourse on the sealing

67

power of the priesthood. He again referred to the Saints as being saviors on Mount Zion and asked: "But how are they to become saviors on Mount Zion? By building their temples, erecting their baptismal fonts, and going forth and receiving all the ordinances, baptisms, confirmations, washings, anointings, ordinations and sealing powers upon their heads, in behalf of all their progenitors who are dead, and redeem them that they may come forth in the first resurrection and be exalted to thrones of glory with them" (*TPJS*, p. 330).

In the context of Obadiah, work for the dead ancestors of Edom will also be done in the temples established through the restoration of the gospel to the house of Joseph in America. Those millions of people of the lineage of Edom, and other surrounding nations who have not had opportunity to hear the gospel in this life, will hear it in the spirit world and will then be saved through the ordinances performed in the temples built in the latter days. President John Taylor said that those who administer in the temples of God "become saviors of their own nation; they administer and operate in their interests of their fathers and their friends and associates."[5] This interpretation of Obadiah and those of Joseph Smith have been repeated throughout the history of the Church. Typical of many such interpretations is the following by Elder Theodore M. Burton:

> Thus, those living today must perform the physical ordinance work on the earth that will qualify persons in the spirit world to receive that proxy work done for them, even as we living today receive the proxy work done for us by Jesus Christ. In other words, we work in partnership here on the earth with those missionaries in the spirit world who preach the gospel of Jesus Christ to those persons living in the spirit world, that they might be judged according to men in the flesh. This combination effort can free them from their spiritual prison and heal their bruised souls through Jesus Christ. This is why the members of the Church who

---

[5]John Taylor *JD*, 21:97.

can qualify through righteous living must go to the temple in ever-increasing numbers and why they must attend the temple more frequently than they have ever done in the past.[6]

Obviously other Old Testament prophets knew of this great work of the latter days, but it is to Obadiah that we turn for biblical confirmation of the concept of the descendants of Joseph, son of Jacob, becoming saviors on Mount Zion through vicarious work for the dead in the latter-day temples. This smallest of biblical writers will be more appreciated by the posterity of Edom as they recognize the contribution he made to an understanding of their future and final message of hope.

---

[6]Theodore M. Burton, CR, October 1970, p. 35.

Jonah – Prophet of Redemption

Jonah is one of the more controversial books of the Bible. Some accept it as an actual account of a real person, while others label it as a myth or allegory.

The arguments over the literalness of the book of Jonah have gone on for hundreds of years and will no doubt continue until the time of the restoration of other records that will shed light on the issue.[1]

Jonah's overall message is that God (Jesus Christ) is the controlling power of the earth. He knows the intents of our hearts and the extent of our travels. Although we have our agency, the Lord has a program to give all the inhabitants of the earth an opportunity to fulfill the measure of their creation. This message is the same whether the book is accepted as literal or allegorical.

Those who look upon the story of Jonah as a figurative or symbolic allegory do so with scriptural justification. In the book of Jeremiah we read, "Nebuchadrezzar the king of Babylon hath devoured me [Judah], he hath crushed me, he hath made me an empty vessel, he hath swallowed me up like a dragon, he hath filled

---

[1]Lehi prophesied that the "plates of brass should go forth unto all nations, kindreds, tongues, and peoples who were of his seed" (1 Nephi 5:18). These plates contained much more information about the Old Testament than does our present Bible, the record being larger than the combined Old and New Testaments, even though it ended at 600 B.C. (1 Nephi 13:23). The book of Kings that mentions the prophet Jonah (2 Kings 14:25) is an abridgment of other records (2 Kings 14:28); therefore more about Jonah might have been contained in the unabridged account. An unabridged account may also have been in the plates of brass.

his belly with my delicates, he hath cast me out (Jeremiah 51:34). Allegorically the great fish that swallowed Jonah would represent Babylon, and Jonah would be the nation of Judah. Judah was taken captive by Babylon in about 607 B.C. and was in bondage for seventy years, until about 538 B.C., as prophesied by the prophet Jeremiah (Jeremiah 25:11). At the end of this time, Cyrus, the new ruler of the world as king of Persia, issued a proclamation allowing the Jewish people to return from Babylon (Ezra 1:1). This return would be symbolic of the fish vomiting up Jonah (Jonah 2:10). This later interpretation is also given in the book of Jeremiah: "I will punish Bel in Babylon, and I will bring forth out of his mouth that which he hath swallowed up: and the nations shall not flow together any more unto him: yea, the wall of Babylon shall fall.

"My people, go ye out of the midst of her, and deliver ye every man his soul from the fierce anger of the Lord" (Jeremiah 51:44–45).

Further support of this symbolic interpretation is cited in the apocryphal book of Tobit. Although this reference may be to another prophecy of Jonah's about Nineveh that is not in our present biblical text, the basic element of the prophecy in the book of Jonah is implied:

> Go to Media, my son, for I fully believe what Jonah the prophet said about Nineveh, that it will be overthrown. But in Media there will be peace for a time. Our brethren will be scattered over the earth from the good land, and Jerusalem will be desolate. The house of God in it will be burned down and will be in ruins for a time.
>
> But God will again have mercy on them, and bring them back into their land; and they will rebuild the house of God, though it will not be like the former one until the times of the age are completed. After this they will return from the places of their captivity, and will rebuild Jerusalem in splendor. And the house of God will be rebuilt there with a glorious building for all generations for ever, just as the prophets said of it.
>
> Then all the Gentiles will turn to fear the Lord God in truth, and will bury their idols.

71

All the Gentiles will praise the Lord, and his people will give thanks to God, and the Lord will exalt his people. And all who love the Lord God in truth and righteousness will rejoice, showing mercy to our brethren.

So now, my son, leave Nineveh, because what the prophet Jonah said will surely happen (Tobit 14:4–8).

Using such evidence, many scholars and laymen dismiss the book of Jonah as a historical account and Jonah as a historical person.

Those who hold to the literalness of the text and the personage of Jonah likewise give scriptural support. On two different occasions, Jesus referred to the teachings of the prophet Jonah as a sign of the Messiah's being killed and buried in the heart of the earth for three days and nights (Matthew 12:38– 41; 16:1–4). The account of Jonah thus becomes a type and shadow of Jesus' death and resurrection. It also bears record of Jesus Christ, as the Lord taught Adam that "all things are created and made to bear record of [Him]" (Moses 6:63). Those who believe in the literalness of Jonah further argue that the Son of God would not use mythology to support the literalness of his death and resurrection.

Both of the above arguments have scriptural support. There is no reason to discard one or the other. The symbolism of Judah being swallowed up by Nebuchadnezzar, or earlier of Israel being swallowed up by Assyria, which would fit the time period of Jonah as a prophet in the time of Jeroboam 2, could certainly have been a message of the book of Jonah. It was also a type and shadow of the Savior's death and resurrection. Scriptures do not have to be limited to a single interpretation. But a prophet named Jonah, son of Amittai, did prophesy during this time period, as verified in 2 Kings 14:25. The superscription of Jonah (1:1) identifies him as the prophet who wrote the Old Testament book called by his name. Therefore, Jonah's authorship of the biblical text is supported by scripture, although it is not yet proven. Someday that proof will undoubtedly come.

The first message of the book of Jonah is taken from the account in chapter 1. Jonah's attempt to flee from his calling of preaching to

72

the people of Nineveh by catching a ship to Tarshish is a clear declaration that a person cannot flee from or hide from God. The whereabouts and activities of every person are always known by the omniscient God. The Lord caused a great wind upon the sea to bring fear upon the mariners. Apparently, he also took advantage of the superstitions of the seamen to get Jonah thrown overboard, and he had prepared a great fish to swallow Jonah. As Alma said, "The Lord worketh in many ways to the salvation of his people" (Alma 24:27).

The second message to be learned from Jonah again centers around the textual problems of the book. Arguments are given against the ability of a whale to swallow a person whole or for someone to be able to live for three days in the stomach of a whale. In response to these questions, the text of Jonah does not say that the fish was a whale but that it was a great fish that God had prepared. The New Testament translations have rendered the fish as a whale. However, there are certain types of whales that can and have swallowed people alive, and there are people who have been swallowed and lived for several days in the belly of a whale.[2] Therefore, it is defensible that Jonah was literally swallowed by a fish, but there are further considerations.

The book of Jonah is written in prose except for Jonah 2:2–9, which is a poem. Much of the criticism leveled against this book is about the improbabilities of the occurrences within a fish's belly as described in these verses. Again, to accept the literalness of the story does not obligate one to accept all of the details of the poem. Could the poem be symbolic of Jonah's experience? Jonah says that he "cried out of the belly of hell" (Jonah 2:2). Could this poem be reflecting the experience of Jonah's spiritual rebirth that actually took place while he was incarcerated in the stomach of the fish? The account is similar to that of Alma, the son of Alma, as related to

---

[2]The most readily available source for Latter-day Saints to confirm the ability of whales to swallow someone whole and for one to live through such an ordeal is found in W. Cleon Skousen's *The Fourth Thousand Years*, pp. 458–563, in the story of James Bartley, who spent thirty-six hours in a whale following a whaling expedition.

his own sons (Alma 36:4–26). Jonah looked to the Lord, as did Alma, to escape from the depths of hell (Jonah 2:4–9; Alma 36:17–23). While Jonah's experience took place within the fish's stomach, Alma's experience was in a state of mortal unconsciousness but in the presence of an angel.[3] Both lives were dramatically changed. The text being poetic only in this instance lends support to this interpretation. Following the poem, the fish's regurgitation of Jonah is recorded in prose (v. 10).

The third chapter reveals a second call for Jonah to go to Nineveh. This time he responded to the call and journeyed the great distance to Nineveh. The text records that "Nineveh was an exceeding great city of three days' journey" (Jonah 3:3). This is interpreted to mean that the city was so large that it took three days to journey from one side of it to the other. Again critics have questioned the validity of the book because excavations by archaeologists have failed to support the existence of such an extensive city. Regardless, let us consider the message of the account. Jonah's message was that within "forty days . . . Nineveh shall be overthrown" (Jonah 3:4). This was apparently a conditional prophecy, although the text does not say it was. The people of Nineveh repented, and a fast was proclaimed in hopes that by their repenting and turning to God, "he [would] turn away from us his fierce anger" (JST, Jonah 3:9). God saw their works and observed that they "repented; and God turned away the evil that he had said he would bring upon them" (JST, Jonah 3:10). This message is repeated in the Book of Mormon: God never destroys a nation unless he first warns them by his prophets (see 2 Nephi 25:9). Jonah was the prophet the Lord had sent to warn Nineveh.

A fourth message of the book is based upon Jonah's reaction to the people's repentance. In spite of acknowledging that God was

---

[3]Other experiences of rebirth similar to Jonah's and Alma's are those of Jacob, father of the house of Israel; and Enos, the son of Jacob, brother of Nephi, as recorded in the Book of Mormon. Jacob's wrestle is recorded in Genesis 32:24–28, but the interpretation is alluded to in Genesis 48:16. Enos's experience is recorded in the Book of Mormon, Enos 1:2–8. A careful study of these two accounts would further support the interpretation that Jonah experienced a spiritual rebirth.

merciful and gracious, Jonah was angry and asked that God take his life. Perhaps Jonah was fearful of the people since his prophecy had not been fulfilled, or perhaps he was embarrassed because of this. The latter seems more probable. All the text says is that God questioned Jonah about his anger. Jonah left the city in his anger and went outside the city, where he built a booth to provide some shade and waited to see what would become of the city (Jonah 4:5). The average temperature today in Nineveh is extremely hot; it is likely that it was anciently as well. To help Jonah learn another great lesson, God caused a gourd to grow, providing shade for Jonah, which he greatly appreciated (Jonah 4:6). Then God prepared a worm that destroyed the gourd and took away Jonah's shade. He then caused a vehement east wind (from off the hot desert) in addition to the already unbearable heat. This resulted in Jonah's fainting and again wishing he would die (John 4:7–8).

Using this very uncomfortable condition, God gave Jonah a combination of lessons. He asked Jonah if he was justified in being angry for the gourd withering up, something that he had had nothing to do with — its planting, growing, or dying. The lesson then came. If Jonah was so concerned over a plant, why wasn't he concerned over the people and the animals in the great city of Nineveh. Jonah had had nothing to do with their being there or their condition either. They were God's concern, and he had sent Jonah to try to rectify the wicked situation that existed there. Rather than rejoice over their repentance, he had pouted over his own pride being hurt because his prophecy was not fulfilled. As a servant of God, he should follow God's will, not his own.

God reminded him of the number of people in the city — one hundred twenty thousand. These people were Gentiles and had not had an opportunity to hear the gospel and did not know the difference between good and evil (could not discern between their right hand and their left hand). Where there was no law, there was no transgression (Romans 4:15). God further reminded Jonah of his concern for the cattle, who were also God's creation. God has a

75

love for all his creations—men and animals—and gives all an opportunity to be saved.

Jonah was a prophet of the Lord Jesus Christ. The Lord used him to bring a great city of thousands of people to repentance. In fulfilling his mission, Jonah was also used as an allegory of the coming death and resurrection of the Lord Jesus Christ, as well as of the future destiny of the nation of Judah. We should emphasize and learn from this important message rather than argue over the reality of the story or the prophet.

Micah: A Second Witness
with Isaiah

The superscription of the book of Micah (Micah 1:1) dates Micah's prophecies in the days of Jotham, Ahaz, and Hezekiah, kings of Judah. A comparison with Isaiah's superscription shows that these two prophets were contemporaries. Isaiah's ministry spanned the last year of Uzziah, the king of Judah who preceded Jotham.[1] How long Micah prophesied during Jotham's reign is not known, but it is safe to assume that Micah's ministry was a little shorter than Isaiah's. Since tradition labels Isaiah as the leading prophet of the time, we can also assume that Micah was under Isaiah's jurisdiction. The time period is around 740 B.C. to 700 B.C.

The superscription also states that Micah "saw concerning Samaria and Jerusalem." Isaiah also prophesied to Jerusalem and Samaria. While Isaiah's superscription mentions only Judah, the context of Isaiah chapter 1, the preface to his book, shows that Isaiah's call was to Samaria, or Northern Israel, also. Although the book of Micah is much shorter than the book of Isaiah, the context of Micah's prophecies are similar and sometimes identical to Isaiah's.

The first prophecy of Micah, recorded in chapter 1, is

---

[1]Actually, Jotham reigned for several years while his father had leprosy, but the exact time is not known.

undoubtedly a dual prophecy, typical of many of Isaiah's prophecies. The two separate time periods for the prophecy are the Assyrian conquest of Samaria in 722 B.C. and the Second Coming of Christ. The Assyrian conquest left "Samaria as an heap of the field, and as plantings of a vineyard" (Micah 1:6). The iniquities of Samaria were "incurable" and had spread over into Jerusalem (Micah 1:5, 9). The same declaration had been made by Isaiah (Isaiah 1:5–8; 8:5–8). However, on this occasion, the mountains were not "molten under [the Lord], and the valleys [were not] cleft, as wax before the fire, and as the waters that are poured down a steep place" (Micah 1:4). While the description of the Lord coming down and treading upon the earth (Micah 1:3) may be symbolic of the Samarian conquest and not a literal treading down, it will be literally fulfilled at the second coming of Christ (see Isaiah 40:3–5 and JST, Luke 3:4–11). Therefore, the dual prophecy seems the most probable explanation of its fulfillment.

The majority of chapter 2 is a more specific pronouncement of Israel's sins: immorality, loss of freedoms, oppression of the poor, and acceptance of false prophets rather than the Lord's prophets. These sins were also enumerated by Isaiah (Isaiah 5:8–24; 9:8–10:4).

A Remnant Shall Return

In manner similar to Isaiah's prophesying, Micah follows his message of doom with a message of hope. Thus, in spite of Israel's destruction, the Lord, through Micah, promises that he will again assemble all of Jacob, or "gather the remnant of Israel" (Micah 2:12). This is a constant theme of Isaiah's writing (see, for example, Isaiah 6:13; 10:20–21, 27). While Micah later enlarges on the gathering prophecy, at this time he continues his analysis of why the destruction was imminent. The first reason was that, as Isaiah had also said, their leaders "caused them to err" (Micah 3:5; Isaiah 9:11). The Lord further declares through Micah that there will be no answer to the leaders' prayers, there will be no vision to the false prophets, "the seers [shall] be ashamed, and the diviners confounded . . . for there is no answer from God" (Micah 3:6–7). Continuing the chastisement, the Lord says that the leaders "judge for reward," "teach for hire," and the prophets "divine for money" and yet claim that the Lord is with them. Under such circumstances, the Lord announces that it is for the people's sake, to rid them of such corrupt leadership, that the Lord is going to plow Zion as a field and leave Jerusalem as a heap (Micah 3:11–12). The corruption has brought destruction, but a remnant will be preserved.

The Last Days

Having foretold the downfall of Samaria and Jerusalem, Micah now turns to several prophecies that will not be fulfilled until the last days. This makes a natural division in the book of Micah. The first three chapters basically refer to the days of Micah, Isaiah, and other prophets, while the last four foretell the Lord's doings in the latter days. Since these prophecies are now being fulfilled, it seems that these chapters are more relevant to us. Of course, the others are important also to give us the background of the prophecies.

The Temple in the Top of the Mountains

The first prophecy of the latter days is one almost identical to Isaiah's prophecy of the building of a temple in the top of the mountains. The difference in the two prophecies is that Isaiah uses it as a time frame for the work of God to commence among the people of Judah in Jerusalem,[2] while Micah uses it as an event to precede the great gathering to Zion from among the Gentiles in the latter days. Of course both usages are related.

As referred to by both Micah and Isaiah, the temple to be built in the top of the mountains has reference to the temple to be built in Independence, Jackson County, Missouri (preface to Doctrine and Covenants 57; 3 Nephi 21:11–23). The top of the mountains is undoubtedly a synonym for "the everlasting hills," as prophesied

---

[2]For a fuller treatise of the Isaiah prophecy, see Monte Nyman, *Great are the Words of Isaiah* (Salt Lake City: Bookcraft, 1980), pp. 26–31.

by Jacob, father of the twelve tribes (Genesis 49:26; see also Deuteronomy 33:13–17). This conclusion is drawn from Jacob's knowledge of the New Jerusalem being built upon this continent, which knowledge he obtained through a covenant with the Lord (3 Nephi 20:22). The law going forth from Zion, stated by both prophets, was identified by President George Albert Smith as the principles of freedom established under the United States Constitution.[3] The word of the Lord coming from Jerusalem is a prophetic declaration that the gospel will someday be preached in Jerusalem.[4] The following verses of the Micah prophecy (4:3–5) describe the ushering in of the Millennium, which will follow shortly after the building of the New Jerusalem. Joseph Smith paraphrased part of verse 4 in support of the gathering of Israel and the Millennium, "when every man may sit under his own vine and fig tree, and there will be none to molest or make afraid" (*TPJS*, p. 93). Isaiah's prophecy also includes the millennial description in almost verbatim language (Isaiah 2:4). In the "Second General Epistle of the Presidency of The Church of Jesus Christ of Latter-day Saints, from the Great Salt Lake Valley, to the Saints Scattered Throughout the Earth," the First Presidency refers to "the dawning of the day when the children of the Kingdom can sit under their own vines and fig-tree and inhabit their own houses, having none to make them afraid."[5] Both Isaiah and Micah then treat the gathering of Israel, but Micah's account is quite different than Isaiah's.

The Gathering to Zion

The temple being built in Jackson County, Missouri, is used in Micah as a time signal that the gathering to that location is under

---

[3]This interpretation was given at the dedication of the Idaho Falls Temple (*Improvement Era*, October 1945; *Ensign*, November 1971, p. 15, as quoted by Harold B. Lee). Dedicatory prayers are given by revelation (see the preface to section 109 in the Doctrine and Covenants).

[4]At present (1990), The Church of Jesus Christ of Latter-day Saints has made a commitment not to preach the gospel or proselyte in Jerusalem. When the gospel is preached, it will be by invitation of that Jewish nation (see Isaiah 26:1–2).

[5]James R. Clark, *Messages of the First Presidency*, 2:32 (Salt Lake City: Bookcraft, 1965).

way. This is concluded from the familiar Old Testament phrase "in that day" (Micah 4:6). In the day when the temple is built, the Lord will gather in from all nations those Israelites who had previously been "driven out" of their promised lands and assemble them in "mount Zion," where he will personally "reign over them" (Micah 4:6–7).

From the Prophet Joseph Smith we learn that the Zion spoken of by the Old Testament prophets is the whole of North and South America (*TPJS*, p. 362). Mount Zion would indicate the height, or the central place, of North and South America, which is designated by revelation as Independence, Missouri (D&C 57:3).

The "strong nation" (Micah 4:7) over which the Lord will reign and which will be made strong by him is the restored nation of Israel. Again Micah supports the concept spoken of in more detail by the prophet Isaiah (Isaiah 55). Christ, "whose right it is to reign," will be there, in Zion, as king (D&C 58:22). His kingdom will first have "dominion" in Zion and then "shall come to the daughter of Jerusalem" (Micah 4:8), the political kingdom that was delivered by the woman (church) in the meridian of time to rule all nations with a rod of iron (word of God), but was caught up to God. The woman (church), driven into the wilderness because of the great red dragon (the devil), will now be delivered from the hands of her enemies and be established (see Revelation 12:1–6 and Micah 4:9–10).

Isaiah likewise predicts the birth of this man-child, the political kingdom of God (Isaiah 66:5–10). Although the kingdom is born, it is born in Babylon, or among the wickedness of the world (D&C 133:14) and will thus be opposed by the world. However, the world knows "not the thoughts of the Lord" (Micah 4:12; compare Isaiah 55:8), and the Lord will gather his people, the house of Israel, out of the world as a thresher in the ancient world gathered the grain "sheaves into the floor" and brought forth the seed of grain from the straw and chaff (Micah 4:13).

The Savior, by the Father's commandment, taught this same concept to the Nephites when he quoted the prophecy of Micah (or Isaiah)⁶ in the context of the gathering of Israel from the Gentiles to establish the New Jerusalem in the Americas in fulfillment of the covenant to his people (3 Nephi 20:12–22). The two witnesses — Micah and Isaiah — of this gathering are thus interpreted and confirmed by the Book of Mormon. The Lord gives a third witness in the appendix to the Doctrine and Covenants and also adds another dimension. In explaining why he restored the fulness of the gospel, the Lord used the terminology of Micah 4:13, "And by the weak things of the earth the Lord shall thrash the nations by the power of his Spirit" (D&C 133:59). The power of the Lord's Spirit will be the major factor in the gathering.

Out of Bethlehem Comes the Ruler in Israel

One of the favorite scriptures from Micah is the prophecy that Christ would be born in Bethlehem. However, most of the people who are familiar with this prophecy fail to put the prophecy into its proper context and thus fail to analyze the entire prophecy. The context of the prophecy is still in the last days, and the subject is still the gathering of the remnant of Israel.

The first verse of the prophecy speaks of the gathering of troops: "O daughter of troops." The "daughter of troops" seems to be the gathering of Israel to Zion and her stakes, similar to the Gentiles who have gathered against Zion. The mother nations (Babylon) gathering against Zion have set the pattern for the daughter (Israel), who has been scattered among them, to gather as a refuge from the threatened Gentile storm (see Isaiah 4:5–6; D&C 115:6). The nations of Babylon will lay siege against Zion and smite the judge of Israel (Christ) with a rod upon the cheek (Micah 5:1). The rod

---

⁶This prophecy was probably originally in the book of Isaiah as well as in the book of Micah. This conclusion is drawn from the fact that Christ speaks repeatedly of the fulfillment of Isaiah's prophecies and never mentions Micah (see 3 Nephi 20:11–12; 23:1–2). Other prophecies of Isaiah are interspersed in the Savior's commentary (see 3 Nephi 16:7–20; 20:32–45; 21:29; 22:1–17). Although the Savior does make general references to the other prophets (3 Nephi 23:5), when he specifically quotes Malachi, he does identify Malachi's writings. With the loss of many plain and precious parts from the record of the Jews (1 Nephi 13:26–29), this theory seems highly plausible.

here seems to be symbolic of a verbal barrage against the people of Zion who are gathering under the direction of the Lord or judge of Israel.

In an apparent explanation of why this will happen in the last days, the Lord, through Micah, refers back to the humble beginning of the "ruler in Israel" in the little town of Bethlehem. He then quickly confirms that this was not the beginning of his rulership, for he had been administering the affairs of the house of Israel "from of old, from everlasting" (Micah 5:2). That this prophecy speaks of Christ's birth is confirmed by two of the New Testament apostles (Matthew 2:6; John 7:42). However, that this is also a prophecy of the last days is clear, for Micah explains that the Lord would give Judah up "until the time that she which travaileth hath brought forth" (Micah 5:3). This refers back to the travailing of Zion to establish the kingdom as prophesied earlier (Micah 4:10). Not until this kingdom is established will the tribe of Judah, "the remnant of his [Christ's] brethren," return unto the children of Israel (Micah 5:3). In other words, the conversions of Judah will not happen until after the building of the New Jerusalem in Missouri (3 Nephi 21:23–29).

Micah then explains how Christ will be Judah's strength against the Gentile nations gathered against her and shall deliver Judah from her oppressors represented as the Assyrians and the land of Nimrod (Micah 5:4–6). Micah concludes his prophecy about Judah with the declaration that a remnant of Jacob shall be among many people, not just the Jewish gathering (Micah 5:7). This declaration sets the stage for the last prophecy recorded in the book of Micah.

The Remnant of Jacob among the Gentiles

The last prophecy of Micah (and Isaiah, see note on p. 82) is quoted in its entirety by the Savior to the Nephites and earlier referred to or partially quoted by him twice more (3 Nephi 21:12–21; 16:13–14; 20:16–17). Much understanding of this prophecy is gained through the Savior's commentary on these three occasions.

The remnant of Jacob who have been scattered among the

83

Gentiles are prophesied to go forth as a lion among a flock of sheep and tread down the Gentiles, who will be their enemies at this time (Micah 5:8–9). The first two times the Savior quotes this prophecy to the Nephites, he makes it a conditional prophecy based upon whether the Gentiles repent. If the Gentiles do repent, they will be numbered among the house of Israel and thus escape being trodden down (3 Nephi 16:13–15; 20:15–17). The Savior's second quotation qualifies the conditional treading down as being caused by the Gentiles' failure to repent after the blessings of the knowledge of the Lord have been revealed to them after they have scattered the house of Israel before them (3 Nephi 16:13–15; 20:15–17). In other words, the Lord will forgive the Gentiles for their treatment of the house of Israel if the Gentiles accept the gospel, which will be restored among them. However, if they reject the gospel, then the mercy of the Father will be withdrawn and justice will take its course.

The third time Christ quotes this prophecy, he quotes it in its entirety, describing the things that will occur among the Gentiles. He also qualifies the condition a little further. Those who do not repent and accept the gospel will be cut off from among the house of Israel and will then be trodden down by the house of Israel. Those who do repent will have the Church established among them, be numbered among the remnant of Jacob to whom this land was given (see 3 Nephi 15:12–13), and assist the remnant of Jacob in building the New Jerusalem (3 Nephi 21:11–12). Thus, the house of Israel will eventually tread down the rebellious Gentiles, but those who repent can escape this treading down if they accept the gospel and are numbered with Israel. This concept is sustained by the modern-day prophecy on war revealed through the Prophet Joseph Smith: "And it shall come to pass also that the remnants who are left of the land will marshal themselves, and shall become exceedingly angry, and shall vex the Gentiles with a sore vexation" (D&C 87:5).

The conditions that will bring about the treading down of the Gentiles by the house of Israel are symbolically represented by Micah. Recognizing that there are other possible interpretations, the following are offered. The Father will cut off from the Gentiles their horses and destroy their chariots (Micah 5:12). This may have reference to the transportation system among the Gentiles. Such things as gasoline shortages or truckers' strikes could certainly cripple a nation that so heavily relies upon transportation.

The cutting off of the cities and throwing down of strongholds suggests a possible breakdown of law enforcement (Micah 5:11). Cities not having help from state or federal sources could bring such a condition.

The Lord will also cut off witchcrafts and soothsayers from the Gentile lands (Micah 5:12). This could suggest the reliance of the Gentiles upon their philosophers, economists, educators, and scientists instead of relying upon the Lord, as well as the literal practice of witchcraft. These factions are certainly among the Gentiles today.

Micah next lists the graven images and other images—the worship of the work of the Gentile hands that will be cut off (Micah 5:13). While the literalness of this type of image worship does exist, only a small percentage of the Gentile population so worship. Therefore, this could more fully refer to the clothes, money, positions, and other worldly things worshiped in our society today.

Last of all, Micah says that the Lord will pluck up the groves out of their midst and destroy their cities (Micah 5:14). Worshipping the pagan god Baal included gathering together in groves to participate in temple prostitution, child sacrifice, and other degenerative rituals. In our societies today, the communes, especially in large cities, where various immoral practices are conducted certainly fit this symbolism.

In the Book of Mormon account, the Savior adds a general description of "all lyings and deceivings, and envyings, and strifes, and priestcrafts, and whoredoms, [that] shall be done away" (3 Nephi 21:19). Perhaps this was originally a part of the text; regardless, it shows that the Lord will cleanse from the Gentiles those things the Gentiles would not cleanse from themselves through repenting and accepting the gospel when it was restored among them.

The Book of Mormon commentary by the Savior also adds

85

another important element to the prophecy—that of a time period. According to the Book of Mormon, the majority of the house of Israel will not be taught the gospel until after the New Jerusalem is built by the house of Israel, assisted by the repentant Gentiles (3 Nephi 21:24–29). Therefore, the treading down of the Gentiles by the house of Israel will be in the times when the Gentiles are fulfilled but before the gospel is fully taken to Israel.[7] The times of the Gentiles being fulfilled is when the Gentiles have rejected the fulness of the gospel and the gospel is brought from them (3 Nephi 16:10; see also JST, Luke 21:24–32; D&C 45:28–33). This also suggests that the house of Israel who are doing the treading down will be those who are not yet taught the gospel and are not the members of the Church. Thus it will be a political or temporal movement by those in rebellion against the mistreatment of the Gentiles who have ruled over them for hundreds of years. This seems consistent also with Joseph Smith's prophecy on war (D&C 85:7). This movement will probably fulfill the promise to Joseph of Egypt that his seed would be brought "out of captivity unto freedom" (2 Nephi 3:5). It may further fulfill a prophecy of father Lehi that one mighty among the seed of his son Joseph would be "an instrument in the hands of God, with exceeding faith, to work mighty wonders, and do that thing which is great in the sight of God, unto the bringing to pass much restoration unto the house of Israel, and unto the seed of thy brethren" (2 Nephi 3:24). That this would be a prophet raised up in the latter days among the Lamanites has been taught by modern-day apostles.[8]

There is one more caution or observation about this prophecy: it should not be limited to the Lamanites or to any one group of the house of Israel.[9] As typical of Isaiah's prophecies (see 3 Nephi

---

[7]Elder Bruce R. McConkie labels the prophecy as millennial and as a part of the second coming of Christ. See *Mortal Messiah*, 4:335–37; 356–57.

[8]Joseph Fielding Smith, *Doctrines of Salvation*, compiled by Bruce R. McConkie, 3 vols. (Salt Lake City: Bookcraft, 1954), 2:251, and Elder Spencer W. Kimball, CR, October 1947, p. 22, have both taught that this is a future Lamanite prophet.

[9]This caution was given by Joseph Fielding Smith, *Doctrines of Salvation*, 2:249–50.

16:17–20; 3 Nephi 20:32–35), this prophecy could have fulfillment among the Lamanites, again among the Jews, and also among others of the house of Israel. Nonetheless, it will be fulfilled, and the Lord "will execute vengeance in anger and fury upon the heathen, such as they have not heard" (Micah 5:15). The Book of Mormon again renders this passage a little plainer. The Lord will "execute vengeance and fury upon them [the Gentile], even as upon the heathen, such as they have not heard" (3 Nephi 21:21). Vengeance is the Lord's and he will repay (see Mormon 3:15).

Although this prophecy has no direct parallel in Isaiah, as noted above, it was probably in the original Isaiah's text (see footnote 6).

The Lord's Controversy with His People Israel

Having foretold the events of the last days, the Lord now turns back to Israel to admonish them of their requirements to be his people. Whether this refers to Israel of the last days or of Micah's day is not certain; perhaps it is both — a dual prophecy. However, the context of chapters 4 and 5 is the last days, and there is no indication of a change of context. Furthermore, the admonition to the mountains also implies that the context is the last days and refers to the land of Joseph, the Americas. Even if it were addressed to ancient Israel, the endless nature of the principles of the gospel make it applicable to our day.

After a review of what the Lord has done for Israel in past times (leading them out of Egypt by Moses, Aaron, and Miriam, and the account of Balaam in the wilderness), the Lord reminds Israel that it is not the ritual of the law that pleases him but rather his requirement "to do justly, and to love mercy, and to walk humbly with thy God" (Micah 6:8). This again reminds us of Isaiah's similar chastisement of Israel in his days (Isaiah 1:10–14). It further refutes the false concept in much of the Christian world that the Old Testament God is a God of justice and the New Testament God is a God of mercy. While the law of Moses was to teach justice, it was also to bring Israel to Christ so that they might receive of his mercy (see Mosiah 13:27–32; Galatians 3:23–29). The gospel in its fulness was taught in Old Testament times, except for the last several hundred years when the law of Moses was added to the gospel (Galatians 3:8).[10] The concepts of justice and mercy are eternal principles of the gospel and are to be properly balanced (see Alma 34:15–16; 42:11–31).

As a continuation of the concept of justice and mercy, the Lord reminds his people how they will know to properly follow these principles: "The Lord's voice crieth unto the city, and the man of wisdom shall see thy name: hear ye the rod, and who hath appointed it" (Micah 6:9). The rod spoken of here seems to be the same servant spoken of in Isaiah 11. Moroni testified that the prophecies in Isaiah 11 would soon be fulfilled (JS–H 1:40). Joseph Smith interpreted the rod as a servant in the hands of God (D&C 113:1–6). The traditional interpretation of Joseph Smith's explanation has been that it refers to Joseph himself or to the prophet of the Church. Thus, in another parallel of Isaiah, Micah teaches us to look to the president of the Church, who was appointed by the Lord for our guidance. Following this positive admonition, the Lord warns of several injustices such as wicked balances and violence of the rich, which will bring desolation and reproach upon his people.

Chapter 7 provides a further description of evil society. This description includes the absence of an upright person, seeking for blood, great evil, lack of trust, and dishonor in the family. The Savior cites some of these verses from Micah (Micah 7:6–7) in warning his apostles of what awaited them in their ministry (Matthew 10:35–36; Luke 12:53). The conclusion drawn by Micah, in light of these conditions, is to "look unto the Lord; I will wait for the God of my salvation: my God will hear me" (Micah 7:7). The message is that in spite of these conditions, the Lord will sustain Israel.

The conclusion of the book of Micah is that Israel should trust in the Lord to plead her cause and deliver her from her enemies.

---

[10]See the Prophet Joseph Smith's enlightening commentary on the concept of the law being added to the gospel and other insights on Galatians 3:8 in *TPJS*, p. 60.

The Lord will show marvelous things, as when he brought Israel out of Egypt. The nations will lick the dust from Israel's feet, another tie-in with Isaiah (see Micah 7:17 and Isaiah 49:23). After praising the Lord's mercy, Micah assures the fulfillment of the covenant made to Jacob and Abraham (Micah 7:19–20). The fulfillment of this covenant is also a constant theme of Isaiah (see Isaiah 10:27; 11:12–15; 27:12–13).

Micah the Morasthite has added his testimony to the great words of Isaiah. The two together, along with others such as Amos and Hosea, fulfill the Lord's law of witnesses that "at the mouth of two witnesses or at the mouth of three witnesses, shall the matter be established" (Deuteronomy 19:15). The acceptance of these witnesses can bring us the blessings of the covenant of Israel and Abraham or the curses of the rebellious Gentiles.

Micah, the Second Witness to Isaiah
The Lord's Law of Witnesses (Deuteronomy 19:15)

Concept	Micah	Isaiah	Other Scriptures
Superscription	1:1	1:1	
Samaria Destroyed	1:5–6, 9	1:5–8; 8:58	
Mountains, Valleys	1:4	40:3–5	JST, Luke 3:4–11
Sins of Israel	2:1–13	5:8–24; 9:8–10:4	
Remnant Return	2:12	6:13; 10:20–21, 27	
Leaders Err	3:5	9:11	
Temple in the Mountains	4:1–3	2:2–4	D&C 57:3; 3 Ne. 21:11–23; 20:22
Strong Nation	4:7	55:1–5	
Political Kingdom	4:9–10	66:5–10	Rev. 12:1–6
Lord's Thoughts	4:12	55:8	
Sheaves into the Floor	4:13		3 Ne. 20:12–22
Gatherer to Zion	5:1	4:5–6	D&C 115:6

89

Concept	Micah	Isaiah	Other Scriptures
Ruler in Israel	5:2		Matt. 2:6; John 7:42
Judah's Return	5:3	3 Ne. 21:23–29	
As a Lion among Sheep	5:8–15	3 Ne. 16:13–15; 20:16–17; 21:12–21; D&C 87:5	
Ritual vs. Justice and Mercy	6:6–8	1:10–14	Mosiah 13:27–32; Gal. 3:23–29
The Rod	6:9	11:1	D&C 113:6
Evil Society	7:6–7		Matt. 10:35–36; Luke 12:53
Lick the Dust	7:17	49:23	
Abraham's Covenant	7:19–20	10:27; 11:12–15; 27:12–13	

Seventh-Century Prophets

Judah existed as a nation for over one hundred and thirty years after the fall of Northern Israel, 721 B.C. to 589 B.C.[1] During this period, eight different kings reigned over the nation. Six of these eight kings were labeled as evil by the writers of Kings and Chronicles. After the first king, Hezekiah, only Josiah, the fourth king, gave Judah good leadership. Thus, Judah followed the pattern of her sister nation Israel by ripening in iniquity, which brought the wrath of God upon her unto destruction (1 Nephi 17:35). A brief analysis of each king's reign illustrates Judah's gradual downfall.

The abbreviated account of Hezekiah's reign (2 Kings 18–20) is also given in Isaiah 36–39 and belongs to a study of the prophet Isaiah.[2] Hezekiah's years finished out the eighth century. His son Manasseh succeeded him and reigned for fifty-five years. Manasseh followed the abominations of the heathen and rebuilt the worship places and altars of Baal that his father had destroyed. These practices

---

[1]The 589 B.C. date for the fall of Judah is based on its occurrence in the eleventh year of Zedekiah's reign (2 Kings 25:1–2) and the commencing of the Book of Mormon record in the first year of the reign of Zedekiah (1 Nephi 1:4). Lehi left Jerusalem 600 years before the birth of Christ (1 Nephi 10:4; 19:8; 2 Nephi 25:19). Although the Book of Mormon does not specify how long Lehi prophesied before he left Jerusalem, we generally assume that his teachings in Jerusalem were during the same year (1 Nephi 1:18–19). The traditional date of the fall of Jerusalem is 586 B.C.

[2]For an analysis of Isaiah 36–39, see Monte S. Nyman, *Great are the Words of Isaiah* (Salt Lake City: Bookcraft, 1980), pp. 129–39.

led the nation of Judah to do more evil than the nations that occupied the land of Canaan before Israel was brought out of Egypt (2 Kings 21:1–9). Manasseh was also guilty of shedding much innocent blood (2 Kings 21:16). The Lord warned Manasseh and the people of Judah through "his servants the prophets" (2 Kings 21:10–16; 2 Chronicles 33:18), but they would not hearken. The Lord therefore brought the captains of the king of Assyria upon Manasseh and carried him captive into Babylon. The afflictions under captivity humbled him; when he repented, the Lord returned him to Jerusalem (2 Chronicles 33:10–19). His repentance probably temporarily preserved the nation from destruction. Amon, the son of Manasseh, replaced his father as king but did evil in the sight of the Lord. After two years he was killed by a conspiracy of his own servants (2 Kings 21:19–24). The land was again ripening for destruction.

The ripening of Judah was sent into recession by an eight-year-old boy king, Josiah, son of Amon. His righteous reign of thirty-one years was highlighted by several significant events. In the eighth year of his reign (age sixteen), "he began to seek after the God of David his father: and in the twelfth year he began to purge Judah and Jerusalem" of Baalism (2 Chronicles 34:1–7). In the thirteenth year, the Lord called Jeremiah to be a prophet and to assist the young king in his reformation (Jeremiah 1:1–2). Zephaniah also prophesied during Josiah's ministry, but the Bible gives no dates of the beginning or end of his ministry (Zephaniah 1:1). Through these two prophets, and probably others, the Lord was establishing his word in the mouth of two or more witnesses (see Deuteronomy 19:15).

In the eighteenth year of Josiah's reign (age twenty-six), Josiah authorized a repair of the temple, the house of the Lord (2 Kings 22:3–7). In gathering the money for temple repair, "Hilkiah the priest found a book of the law of the Lord given to Moses" (2 Kings 22:8; 2 Chronicles 34:14). The book was delivered to Shaphan, Josiah's scribe, who delivered it to the king. Upon reading the book, Josiah recognized the failure of his people to live by what was revealed to Moses, and he was greatly troubled. He sent messengers to Huldah, a prophetess of whom little else is known, to inquire of the Lord concerning Judah's status in the eyes of the Lord. The prophetess inquired and learned of the impending destruction upon Judah but gave comfort to king Josiah that it would not come in his day (2 Kings 22:9–20). Obviously encouraged by the messengers' report, the king gathered his people together, read all the words of the newly found book to his people, and made a personal covenant "to walk after the Lord, and keep his commandments" as they were written in the book (2 Kings 23:1–3). He then caused all of Judah and Benjamin (the inhabitants of the nation of Judah) to enter into the same covenant (2 Chronicles 34:32). Josiah followed through on his covenant by removing everything from the land that pertained to the worship of Baal (2 Kings 23:4–20; 2 Chronicles 34:33).

Much speculation has arisen over the account of the discovery of the book of the law of the Lord revealed to Moses. What was that book? Was this the origin of scripture canonization? These and other similar questions, while interesting, are not within the scope of this work. They will be left to another's discussion or analysis of Bible content. The emphasis here is the reformation brought about by Josiah, king of Judah.

There was one more event initiated by Josiah. The passover was kept "as it was written in the book of this covenant." How diligent Israel had been in keeping the passover is not known, but Josiah instituted the keeping of the passover as it had not been kept since the days of Samuel the prophet (2 Kings 23:21–23; 2 Chronicles 35:1–19).

The author of 2 Kings states that there was "no king before [Josiah], that turned to the Lord with all his heart, and with all his soul, and with all his might, according to all the law of Moses; neither after him arose there any like him" (2 Kings 23:25). In spite of his leadership, the seeds of sin sown by Manasseh were deeply entrenched in the people of Judah: "And the Lord said, I will remove Judah also out of my sight, as I have removed Israel, and will cast off this city Jerusalem which I have chosen, and the house of which I said, My name shall be there" (2 Kings 23:27).

Josiah was killed in battle against Necho, king of Egypt. This probably hastened the time of the Lord's threatened destruction. His death brought great sorrow and lamentation to the prophet Jeremiah (2 Chronicles 35:20–25). The Lord had raised them both up to give Judah an opportunity to repent. Although they were effective to some degree, the ripening in iniquity would continue under the next four kings.

Two of the last four kings reigned for only three months each. The other two coincidentally reigned for eleven years each. Jehoahaz the son of Josiah was the first to reign for three months. There is no record of what he did in his short tenure other than evil as his fathers had done. This implies Baalism. He was captured and taken to Egypt and was replaced by another son of Josiah, Eliakim, who reigned for eleven years. His name was changed to Jehoiakim by the king of Egypt, whose servant or puppet king he became. After three years Jehoiakim rebelled against Egypt but was taken captive by Nebuchadnezzar of Babylon and was his puppet king. The Babylonian captivity resulted in many of Judah's people being carried into captivity there. Among the first group of captives was a young man named Daniel, whom the Lord raised up as a prophet to the people of exile (Daniel 1:1).

Jehoiakim was replaced as puppet king by his son Jehoiachin but after three months was taken to Babylon with other Jewish captives. Among this group of ten thousand was another young man named Ezekiel, who was, like Daniel, called to be a prophet to the exiled people (Ezekiel 1:1–3). Another son of Josiah, Mattaniah, whose name was changed to Zedekiah, became the puppet king for the next eleven years. After eleven years, the prophecies of Jeremiah were fulfilled, and Judah as a nation was destroyed and taken captive into Babylon (Jeremiah 25:1–7). The long prophesied event had taken place. Judah had become ripe in iniquity, and the Lord removed her out of his sight as the prophets had warned.

The Vision of Nahum Concerning Nineveh

The prophet Nahum has received little attention from The Church of Jesus Christ of Latter-day Saints, either by its members or its prophets. The Prophet Joseph Smith made no changes to Nahum's writings in his translation of the Bible.[1] Nahum is rarely, if ever, quoted in the conferences of the Church. The brevity of the book may be a factor. It contains only three short chapters covering less than three pages. We know little of Nahum or the historical setting in which he prophesied.

Nineveh, the city to whom this message of doom and destruction is delivered, was the capital city of the ancient Assyrian empire. The destruction of the city is traditionally dated as 712 B.C. and came at the hands of Nabopolassar, the father of Nebuchadnezzar, king of Babylonia. The dating of the book of Nahum is therefore placed somewhere prior to this captivity. The prophet is called an Elkoshite in the superscription of the book (Nahum 1:1), but nothing more is known about the writer and his background.

There is no religious theme or message to the book except the pronounced downfall of the city, although it is considered to be very good poetic literature. Some commentators see the book in the role of dual prophecy, the first destruction being symbolic of the destruction of the Gentiles in the latter days. The first chapter is a

---

[1]There is one slight change in the 1944 edition of the JST in Nahum 1:8. The source of this change is questionable and is insignificant.

praise to God's destructive attributes that will soon come upon Nineveh and to his merciful deliverance of his people. The second chapter describes the city's downfall, and the third chapter tells why it was destroyed. The specifics of each chapter will follow.

The first six verses of chapter 1 describe the Lord's justice and his ability to bring destruction. Although he is slow to anger, the implied cause of the coming destruction is that his patience has run out and he cannot "acquit the wicked" for their sinful nature (Nahum 1:3). There are none of those wicked who can stand before his indignation when he decrees what is to happen (Nahum 1:6).

The next five verses (Nahum 1:7–11) give some comfort to the righteous who are among the wicked (see 1 Nephi 17:37). Nahum says that God is good and knows those who trust in him (Nahum 1:7). In spite of these good people, the majority of the people are evil (Nahum compares them to thorns) and drunkards and will be devoured as stubble (Nahum 1:10). The people also have a very wicked leader who is fighting against the Lord (Nahum 1:11). This wickedness could be described as being "ripened in iniquity" because it is the cause of a people being destroyed (Genesis 15:16; 1 Nephi 17:35). Nineveh's doom has been sealed.

In typical fashion, the Lord reveals to Nahum the message of hope that always follows the message of doom (Nahum 1:12–14). To whom this message is addressed is not clear, but since chapter 2 refers to Jacob and Israel, the message may be addressed to those Israelites who were taken into captivity by Assyria in 721 B.C.

A possible interpretation of Nahum 1:12 is that the italicized words "they be," which were added by the King James translators, had reference to those captive Israelites. The description of their being quiet describes their captivity. Though their captors are many, yet they will be cut down by the invading Nabopolassar. However, the captured Israelites will not be further afflicted. The Assyrian yoke is to be broken off from captive Israel, and no more of her people are to be sown among the Gentiles.[2] The Lord had commanded

---

[2] As prophesied by Amos, the Lord was to sift the house of Israel among all the nations of the earth (Amos 9:8–9).

that Israel was now to be taken as a group into the North, as recorded in 2 Esdras. There they would have the worship of false gods removed from them and there they would eventually go into spiritual death or oblivion because of a yet future apostasy.[3] The lost tribes of Israel would then remain in their apostate condition until God again sent his prophets to publish the good tidings of the restored gospel and to bring peace to them wherever they were at that time. Also in typical Old Testament fashion, Nahum adds a message of hope for Judah, the other place of the latter-day gathering of the house of Israel. As Judah returns to her original solemn feasts (righteous living) and performs her vows (keeps the covenants she would again enter), the wicked will no longer tread her down but will be utterly cut off (Nahum 1:15). Thus, the Lord's long-range plans were revealed through Nahum.

The second chapter describes the destruction of Nineveh and is a type of the destruction to take place in the last days. This conclusion is drawn from the descriptions of chariots with flaming torches that rage in the streets and jostle one against another. The chariot combat of ancient times is supposedly used to describe the tanks and other armored vehicles with modern lighting systems (Nahum 2:3–4). While this is all plausible, verse 2 also has an important message. In the days of the Nineveh captivity, the Lord had taken away the excellency of Jacob, at least from the northern kingdom of Israel. The "emptiers" having "emptied them out" seems to refer to their being taken not only out of the habitat of their promised land but also out of Assyria and into the North, as suggested above. That the verse is primarily a prophecy of the latter days is supported by the last phrase of the verse: the branches of the vine

---

[3]As quoted in chapter 2, 2 Esdras records the taking of the ten lost tribes into the Northland. While this is from the Apocrypha, the Lord has revealed that there are many truths contained in the Apocrypha and that they should be studied with the Spirit. That there was a group taken away that remained intact until at least after the time of Jesus' earthly ministry is confirmed in 3 Nephi 17:1–4. That they later went into apostasy is confirmed by the allegory of the olive tree revealed to Zenos and recorded in the Book of Mormon. Christ and his servant's visit to the olive branches in the latter days, that would have included the lost ten tribes, discloses that none of the branches were at that time producing fruit (Jacob 5:38–39).

have been marred (Nahum 2:2). If this is a sequential prophecy, the marring following the emptying out would be the apostasy following Christ's visit in the meridian of time. This interpretation would allow the chariots with lights and jostling in the streets to be a description of the Gentiles warring among themselves after the times of their opportunity to hear the gospel, as described by the prophet Isaiah (Isaiah 49:25–26; compare 1 Nephi 22:13–14). Thus the Ninevites represent the latter-day Gentiles, and the destruction described also symbolizes the destruction of the Gentiles in the times of their fulness, when they reject the fulness of the gospel and the gospel is taken from them. The Spirit thus withdraws, and they are left to war among themselves (see 3 Nephi 16:10; D&C 45:29–31).

The "worthies" that are recounted in Nahum 2:5 are the leaders. The Lord holds the destinies of all nations in his hand (D&C 117:6), and the wicked leaders of the Gentiles will be removed. The next several verses describe the literal destruction of ancient Nineveh. Huzzab is the queen of Nineveh. The lions probably represent the royalty of Assyria—the king and the princes. All of these leaders and the city were to be ravaged and spoiled in ancient fashion (2:6–12).

The chapter concludes with a declaration that the Lord has decreed this terrible destruction and that he has also withdrawn his messengers, the prophets (Nahum 2:13). The same will be true of the latter-day destruction and withdrawal of the missionaries from among the Gentiles as they reject the gospel (see 3 Nephi 16:10).

The causes of the forthcoming destruction are outlined in chapter 3. The first cause is the lies and the robbery that flourish in the bloody city (Nahum 3:1–3). The second cause is immorality (Nahum 1:4). This is more than sexual immorality, which, of course, will itself destroy a nation (Jacob 3:3, 6). Nineveh's immorality extends to the worship of witchcrafts or false gods (Nahum 3:4). Assyria had apparently been offered the gospel through the captive Israelites, a possible Gentile graft (Jacob 5:7). This offer would symbolically represent a marriage with Jehovah, but she chose to worship the false gods of her various witchcrafts. The Lord announces that he will disclose her immoral practices to the nations and kingdoms of the world. This disclosure is probably the evidence that Nineveh's false gods cannot save her against the only true and living God, Jehovah (Nahum 3:5–7). The Lord uses the ancient Egyptian city of No as an example of what will happen to Nineveh, thus illustrating how fruitless her efforts to prevent the destruction will be (Nahum 3:8–18).

The final decree may also have dual meaning. Nineveh will be scattered, never to be gathered again. The bruise will not heal, the wound will be grievous (Nahum 3:19). While a modern-day city, Mosul, has been built nearby, the ancient Nineveh is still a desolate ruin in the desert. Likewise, when the Gentiles reject the gospel, the Lord will take the gospel to Israel (3 Nephi 16:11–12). The Lord will have fulfilled his promise that the first to receive the gospel in the meridian of time (Israel) will be last to receive it in the latter days; and the last to receive the gospel in the meridian of time (the Gentiles) will be the first to receive it in the last days. While the book of Nahum has been ignored by most Latter-day Saints, there is an important message in its brief record.

Habakkuk: The Lord Is in His Holy Temple

Everyone at some time wonders whether God is aware of and concerned with his or her life. As a person is given more responsibility for the lives of other people, that question enlarges to one of how involved God is or will become in the lives of those over whom he or she has jurisdiction.

The book of Habakkuk answers that question with a declaration that "the Lord is in his holy temple": he is on the job and in full control. Therefore the inhabitants of the earth should "keep silence before [God]." They should listen to and obey his voice rather than question his involvement (Habakkuk 2:20). The historical setting for this great teaching illustrates when and why Habakkuk posed this question and how it was answered.

The book of Habakkuk has no time period given in its superscription. It merely states that it is "the burden [message of doom] which Habakkuk the prophet did see" (Habakkuk 1:1). It is generally assumed that Habakkuk is writing about the conquest of Judah by Nebuchadnezzar king of Babylon. This took place about the seventh year of the reign of Jehoiakim, king of Judah. Egypt under Pharaoh-nechoh had captured Judah after the death of Josiah, king of Judah. The pharaoh carried Jehoahaz captive into Egypt and appointed Jehoahaz's brother Jehoiakim as puppet king (2 Kings 23:31–35). In the fourth year of Jehoiakim's reign, Nebuchadnezzar

100

defeated Egypt and conquered Judah. Jehoiakim became the puppet king to Nebuchadnezzar for three years and then rebelled against him (2 Kings 24:1; Jeremiah 25:1). Nebuchadnezzar then sent bands of Chaldeans, Syrians, Moabites, and Ammonites against Judah to destroy it (2 Kings 24:2).

The traditional dating of this conquest is around 605 B.C. Habakkuk, along with Jeremiah, could possibly be one of the prophets God raised up to warn against the conquest of Babylon (2 Kings 24:2–4; Jeremiah 25:1–2).

A second dating of Habakkuk's warning message could be Nebuchadnezzar's conquest and destruction of Jerusalem in the eleventh year of Zedekiah about nineteen years later (589 B.C. Book of Mormon dating or 586 B.C. traditional dating). The content of Jeremiah 25 would suggest this later date. Either date is drawn from the Lord's reference to his raising up the Chaldeans in answer to a question posed by Habakkuk (Habakkuk 1:1–6). Either date also makes Habakkuk a second witness with Jeremiah to the prophesied conquest of Jerusalem.

That Habakkuk has been prophesying for some time is implied by his opening statement, "O Lord, how long shall I cry, and thou wilt not hear" (Habakkuk 1:2). Habakkuk is apparently perplexed. He has observed the wickedness of the people. He has repeatedly warned them, and yet the Lord has as yet done nothing about it (Habakkuk 1:2–4). Jeremiah had had similar feelings (Jeremiah 20:7–13).

The Prophet Joseph Smith also cried out in like manner against the suffering of the Saints in Missouri (D&C 121:1–6). From the Prophet Joseph's writings, we learn that "when the heart is sufficiently contrite, then the voice of inspiration" comes in answer to the prophet's query (HC 3:293). We therefore assume that as Habakkuk humbled himself, he received the Lord's response to his question.

The Lord revealed to Habakkuk: "Behold ye among the heathen, and regard, and wonder marvelously: for I will work a work in your days, which ye will not believe, though it be told you" (Habakkuk

101

1:5). Although the Prophet Joseph Smith made no changes in this passage as he translated the Bible,[1] "your days" does not refer to Habakkuk's day alone. The work that the Lord referred to was to be fulfilled in the latter days among the heathen or Gentile nations, as shown in the Book of Mormon. The Lord is obviously quoting or paraphrasing Habakkuk, or another prophet who taught the same principle, to the Nephites when he stated: "For in that day, for my sake shall the Father work a work, which shall be a great and a marvelous work among them; and there shall be among them those who will not believe it, although a man shall declare it unto them" (3 Nephi 21:9). The context of the Savior's quotation to the Nephites shows this marvelous work to be the bringing forth of the Book of Mormon by the Prophet Joseph Smith (3 Nephi 21:1–11).

Paul also quoted this verse in the synagogue at Antioch as evidence that Christ and the higher law would not be believed and as a warning against their rejecting him (Acts 13:40–41). Paul did not, however, say that the events of his day fulfilled the prophecy.

From the inspired Book of Mormon text, we can see that the Lord is revealing to Habakkuk that even in the last days there will be those who refuse to listen to the Lord's word revealed through his prophets. From this interpretation can also be drawn some insight in the first phrase of the Lord's answer to Habakkuk, "Behold ye among the heathen." The Lord seems to be saying that evil will not be limited to Habakkuk's day, but that there will be evil in the world as long as Israel lives among the heathens or the Gentiles. The balance between justice and mercy will not be attained until the end of this mortal probation. That the Lord was covering such a broad concept of time is supported by the translation of a commentary on Habakkuk found among the Dead Sea Scrolls. The commentator gave his interpretation that the verse had reference to Habakkuk's own day and to future times, even to the last days

---

[1]Joseph Smith made no corrections in his inspired translation of the Bible in the book of Habakkuk. Because there are differences between Habakkuk 1:5 and the Savior's quotation of it in 3 Nephi 21:9, Joseph apparently did not have sufficient time to carefully review the book of Habakkuk in his translation work.

or the final age when God would appoint a priest to interpret the words of the prophets. This latter-day interpreter we know today to be Joseph Smith:

> This refers to the traitors who have aligned themselves with the man of lies. For they did not believe what he who expounded the Law aright told them on the authority of God. It refers also to those who betrayed the new covenant, for [the word rendered "believe" also means "keep faith" and therefore alludes to the fact that] they have not kept faith with the Covenant of God, but have profaned His holy name. Again, it refers to future traitors — that is, to the lawless men who will betray the Covenant and not believe when they hear all the things that are to come upon the final age duly related by the priest whom God appoints to interpret in those days all the words of His servants the prophets by whom He has told of that impending disaster.[2]

Following the long-range answer to the question of why the Lord allows evil to continue, the Lord then revealed to Habakkuk what he is going to do about the present situation. He will raise up the Chaldeans (Babylonians) and allow them to march through the breadth of the land of Judah and possess it. The Lord then further describes the terribleness of the Chaldeans and their earthly power (Habakkuk 1:5–11). Thus the present evil of such great concern to Habakkuk will be put to an end.

The Lord's answer, however, raises another serious question in the mind of Habakkuk. The prophet begins his question by asking about the eternal nature of God: "Art thou not from everlasting, O Lord my God, mine Holy One?" He then adds the comment that "we shall not die," which seems to be a declaration that the people will not be utterly destroyed but that the Lord is using the Chaldeans to bring judgment and correction upon the nation (Habakkuk 1:12). Using Hebrew parallelism, the same thought is repeated in the second line. Habakkuk acknowledged that God's eyes are "purer

---

[2]Theodor H. Gaster, *The Dead Sea Scriptures*, p. 244.

than to behold evil, and canst not look on iniquity" and then asks his second major question, "Wherefore lookest thou upon them that deal treacherously, and holdest thy tongue when the wicked devoureth the man that is more righteous than he?" (Habakkuk 1:13). To paraphrase the question, Habakkuk is asking why God is using a people who are more wicked than the people of Judah to destroy the nation of Judah? He continued by comparing the people of Judah to fish being caught by men who are representative of the Babylonians (Habakkuk 1:14–17). Showing a determination to receive an answer to his question, even if he is chastised, Habakkuk declares: "I will stand upon my watch, and set me upon the tower, and will watch to see what [God] will say unto me, and what I shall answer when I am reproved" (Habakkuk 2:1). It is not recorded how long he had to wait, but it is unlikely that he waited long before the Lord answered.

The Lord, in his answer, first commanded Habakkuk to "write the vision, and make it plain upon tables, that he may run that readeth it" (Habakkuk 2:2). The interpretation of this passage seems to be that what Habakkuk is about to have revealed to him is to be recorded for future readers and recorded in a manner that the reader will be able to speedily read and understand the message. The Dead Sea Scrolls have another interesting commentary: "God told Habakkuk to write down the things that were to come upon the latter age, but He did not inform him when that moment would come to fulfillment."[3] Although this commentary is not scripture, it is consistent with the text.

The following verse also implies that the "vision" has reference to a future time. The verse reads, "For the vision is yet for an appointed time, but at the end it shall speak, and not lie: though it tarry, wait for it; because it will surely come, it will not tarry" (Habakkuk 2:3). The scroll gives this commentary: "This refers to the fact that the final moment may be protracted beyond anything which the prophets have foretold, for God moves in a mysterious

---

[3]Gaster, pp. 247–48.

104

way His wonders to perform. . . . This is addressed to the men of truth, the men who carry out the Law [Torah], who do not relax from serving the Truth, even though the final moment be long drawn out. Assuredly, all the times appointed by God will come in due course, even as He has determined in His inscrutable wisdom."[4] Again, this commentary seems to suggest the truth that justice is not always observable or immediate or perhaps not even met in this life, but in the end justice will take its course and the results will be according to the eternal truths of the eternal God.

The Lord reassured Habakkuk that "his soul which is lifted up is not upright in him: but the just shall live by his faith" (Habakkuk 2:4). To again paraphrase, a person who pretends to be upright but is not upright in the Lord will have his day of reckoning before the Lord. It is basically the same teaching as given by Jesus that "every one who exalteth himself shall be abased; and he that humbleth himself shall be exalted" (Luke 18:14). The last concept is usually attributed to Paul but is probably quoted from Habakkuk by Paul in his writings, "but the just shall live by his faith" (Habakkuk 2:4; see Romans 1:17; Galatians 3:11; Hebrews 10:3–4). The Lord is telling Habakkuk to not worry about justice in this life, for those who will be justified in the end are those who live by the faith that in the eternal end justice will be met. Salvation is an individual matter, and each person will be judged by how he or she deals with trials and tribulations in this life. As Paul wrote to the Romans, salvation comes to Jew and Gentile as they believe and grows from faith to faith (Romans 1:16–18). To the Galatians, Paul taught that people were not justified by the law (of Moses), that is, by the external meeting of physical commandments, but that salvation came through faith in what the law of Moses represented, the type and shadow of Christ as taught in the law (Galatians 3:10–12, 24). In Hebrews, he[5] uses both verses 3 and 4 to illustrate living by faith until the time of Christ's coming. When properly understood, the

---

[4]Gaster, p. 248.

[5]The controversy over the author of Hebrews being Paul will not be considered here.

gospel as taught in the Old Testament is the same as that taught in the New Testament.

The Lord follows his profound teachings to Habakkuk with several examples and warnings of how justice will eventually be exercised upon those who appear to be prospering in this life. The first example is of a man who is fond of alcohol and neglects his home yet gathers to himself much from all nations and subjects many people to him. The Lord declares that all these things will witness against him in the end (Habakkuk 2:5–8). The second example is of a man who covets earthly possessions and trusts in these riches to keep him from the evils of the world. These things he has acquired at the expense of other people, and these possessions will testify against him at the last day (Habakkuk 2:9–11). The third example is of a man who builds himself a political empire through blood and iniquity and involves many other people in his empire. The conclusion is that knowledge of the Lord is the most prized possession, "for the earth shall be filled with the knowledge of the glory of the Lord, as the waters cover the sea" (Habakkuk 2:12–14). This message was also given by Isaiah as a millennial condition (Isaiah 11:9).[6] The fourth example is a warning to the man who influences his neighbors to indulge in wickedness so that he may take advantage of them. The Lord's wrath will come upon him (Habakkuk 2:15–17). The final warning is to the man who makes or worships graven images. The revelation then concludes: "But the Lord is in his holy temple: let all the earth keep silence before him" (Habakkuk 2:20).

The Lord does not operate through graven images. The Lord dwells in his holy temple and is an all-knowing and perfectly just God. All earthly philosophies and powers will someday acknowledge

---

[6]The knowledge that will fill the earth with the glory of the Lord is his records of eternal truths that he has periodically revealed to mankind. The primary record will be the sealed portion of the records delivered by Moroni to Joseph Smith that were not translated into the Book of Mormon (D&C 5:4–9). For a more complete account of various records that will be available in the Millennium, see Nyman, *Great are the Words of Isaiah*, (Salt Lake City: Bookcraft, 1980), p. 73.

his omniscience and his power and keep silent in awe of him. Those who will learn to do so now will be justified in the day of judgment.

The final chapter of Habakkuk is written as a prayer upon Shigionoth. "Shigionoth is a musical instruction meaning perhaps 'free,' 'diverse'; it would have implications to the performer like 'ad lib.' Selah (vv. 3, 9, 13) is thought to make places where the chanting could make certain liturgical breaks. In any case, the subject and purpose of the song is to praise the Lord."[7] The prayer basically acknowledges that God is a just God.

Habakkuk begins his prayer with a declaration that upon hearing the Lord's answer to his question he was afraid. Probably this fear came because of his realization of the greatness of God and his own weakness. The word *afraid* might better be translated as "awed" or "overcome." He pleads for the Lord to remember or show forth some mercy in the midst of the forthcoming justice of wrath upon Judah. He acknowledges the Lord's involvement in his dealings with the people of Israel in the past and his power over the earth and the elements of the earth (Habakkuk 3:3–12). He further acknowledges that the Lord's actions have always been for the salvation of his children (Habakkuk 3:13–15). Habakkuk again describes his reactions to the Lord's speech and pleads for the Lord's blessings when the prophesied conquest comes upon his people (Habakkuk 3:15). He further declares that no matter what happens—whether the crops fail or the animals are lost—he will rejoice in the Lord, the God of his salvation. He knows that the Lord God is his strength and the source of his blessings. He wants the chief singer to proclaim these thoughts on his stringed instruments (Habakkuk 3:17–19).

The Lord's message to Habakkuk is one that all people must learn. Just as everyone asks questions about God's involvement in his or her life, all will someday learn or be forced to acknowledge that God is in his temple and is in command and controlling the final outcome of the earth and its inhabitants. This answer he has

---

[7]Ellis T. Rasmussen, *An Introduction to the Old Testament and Its Teachings*, part 2, Brigham Young University Press, 1967.

periodically revealed to other servants. Through the Psalmist he said, "Be still, and know that I am God: I will be exalted among the heathen, I will be exalted in the earth" (Psalm 46:10). To Joseph Smith's question of why the Saints suffered in Missouri, he responded, "My son, peace be unto thy soul; thine adversity and thine afflictions shall be but a small moment; and then if thou endure it well, God shall exalt thee on high; thou shalt triumph over all thy foes" (D&C 121:7–8). Earlier he had revealed to Joseph in the form of a question, "Do I not hold the destinies of all the armies of the nations of the earth?" (D&C 117:6). It is better that we learn this lesson from the experience of Habakkuk and others than from the sadness of our own pride and conceit.

Zephaniah: A Second Witness with Jeremiah

The Book of Mormon promises that in the last days the Jews will begin to gather to Jerusalem as they begin to believe in Christ. As they fully believe in Christ, they will complete their gathering and become a delightsome people (2 Nephi 30:7; 3 Nephi 20:29–42). The book of Zephaniah teaches these same promises and outlines the sequence of these happenings from Zephaniah's time until those promises are fulfilled, which will be sometime in the Millennium. Other Old Testament prophets bear testimony of various parts of Zephaniah's prophecy, but he it is who provides a brief overview of the main movements.

Zephaniah prophesied in the days of Josiah, king of Judah. Josiah reigned thirty-one years in Jerusalem and was a good king, the last of the good kings before the downfall of Jerusalem in 589 B.C. (Book of Mormon dating). The next four kings—Jehoahaz, Jehoiakim, Jehoiachin, and Zedekiah—are all labeled as evil in the sight of the Lord (2 Kings 23:17–24:19). Jeremiah began his ministry in the thirteenth year of Josiah's reign and prophesied also during the reigns of the four evil kings. He is considered to be the chief prophet of that period (Jeremiah 1:2–3). During which years of Josiah's reign Zephaniah prophesied is not stated, although his ministry apparently ended before Jeremiah's because no other kings are mentioned in Zephaniah's records.

109

Josiah began to seek the Lord in the eighth year of his reign, and he began to purge Judah of her wickedness in the twelfth year (2 Chronicles 34:3–6). The Lord apparently raised up Jeremiah to assist Josiah in this reformation, and since the Lord always establishes his word in the mouth of two or three witnesses, Zephaniah and Habakkuk were called to serve as those other witnesses. There may have been others as well.

Zephaniah is considered by some to be of royal lineage since the superscription traces his genealogy to Hizkiah (Hezekiah). Whether this Hezekiah is the previous king of Judah is an assumption that has not been proven. Another priest by the name of Zephaniah mentioned in 2 Kings 25:18 (see also Jeremiah 21:1; 37:3) is not the same as the prophet. The prophet's message is more important than his genealogy.

The opening statement of Zephaniah's prophecy is "I will utterly consume all things from off the land, saith the Lord" (Zephaniah 1:2).

Perhaps Zephaniah was one of the many prophets who were warning Judah in the days prior to Lehi's departure (1 Nephi 1:4; 2 Chronicles 36:15–16). Zephaniah is often associated with the invasion of the Scythians, a barbarous group from southern Russia who had affiliated with Assyria just prior to her downfall as the world power and her conquest by the Babylonians. His ministry should not be limited to this invasion, however. The opening prophecy sounds more like the coming Babylonian destruction than the Scythian threat that never materialized. It also suggests more than the Babylonian conquest in verse 3, which speaks of the consumption of man and beast. This wording has led some to suggest that it is a description of the Second Coming. The chapter heading to Zephaniah 1 in the LDS version of the King James Bible indicates that "the destruction of Judah is a type of the second coming." The wording of verse 4, "I will also stretch out mine hand upon Judah, and upon all the inhabitants of Jerusalem," suggests another possibility. Zephaniah is using the already known prophesied destruction that will occur at Christ's second coming as an attention getter before delivering his message of destruction to Judah. Although the setting for the opening prophecy is uncertain, the message to Judah is more specific concerning the cause of their destruction—the worship of Baal and other false gods, and the forsaking and ignoring of the Lord (Zephaniah 1:4–6).

Zephaniah then returns to the Second Coming prophecies and uses them as an example of a similar destruction upon Judah as he speaks of the day of the Lord being at hand (Zephaniah 1:7). In this verse, the bidding of guests to the sacrifice the Lord has prepared is similar to the parable of the great supper (Luke 14:15–24) or the parable of the marriage of the king's son (Matthew 22:1–4), both referring to the Second Coming. Assuming these verses have reference to the Second Coming, the following verses (8–10), introduced with phrases such as "in the same day," are bringing the present audience of Zephaniah back to their own day. Verse 8 speaks of those clothed with strange apparel (Zephaniah 1:8). This is similar to the Matthew parable. Perhaps there were other similar parables at one time in the Old Testament before the plain and precious parts were removed (1 Nephi 13:24–29), and Zephaniah is thus merely referring to things that already had been taught. He again becomes more specific geographically about the destruction that is pending. He warns those who do not acknowledge the hand of the Lord in their lives, saying that "the Lord will not do good, neither will he do evil" (Zephaniah 1:9–12).

Once more Zephaniah uses latter-day prophecies to illustrate the coming destruction of the goods and houses of his own people. As Isaiah had prophesied that in the Millennium people would build houses and inhabit them and plant vineyards and eat the fruit of them (Isaiah 65:22), so Zephaniah specifies that just the opposite was to occur with the people of Judah (Zephaniah 1:13). The great day of the Lord was near for the people of Judah. It would be a day of wrath, trouble, distress, and darkness for them just as the Second Coming will be for the people in the last days (Zephaniah 1:14–16). These conditions would come because the people had sinned against the Lord, and their silver and gold would not be able to deliver them (Zephaniah 1:17–18). Thus Zephaniah is using the prophecies of the destruction of the wicked at the Lord's second coming to warn his present generation of their nation's coming destruction because of their collective wickedness.

Having foretold of the coming destruction, Zephaniah invites those who had been and will be scattered at the time of the destruction to now gather: "Gather yourselves together, yea, gather together, O nation not desired" (Zephaniah 2:1). The "nation not desired" apparently refers to the nation of Judah but may in the broader sense refer to all the house of Israel. Both gatherings will be "before the day of the Lord's anger come upon you" (Zephaniah 2:2). Those who are meek and seek the Lord may "be hid in the day of the Lord's anger" (Zephaniah 2:3). As Isaiah had foretold, the Lord will gather his people together and protect them from the destruction of the wicked (Isaiah 4:5–6). Clearly Zephaniah is again speaking of the Second Coming and the time immediately preceding this advent.

Continuing a description of the period prior to the Second Coming, Zephaniah prophesies about the land surrounding Judah. He first foretells of the cities and peoples of the seacoast: Gaza, Askelon, Ashdod, and Ekron, the land of the Philistines. He prophesies that a remnant of Judah will be freed from their captivity and occupy this land (Zephaniah 1:4–7).[1]

The next prophecy is about Moab and Ammon, the countries traditionally settled by Lot's daughters and lying east of the Jordan River, the present-day nation of Jordan. These two countries were to have destruction and perpetual desolation because they had reproached and magnified themselves against the people of the Lord (Zephaniah 2:8–11). The time of the prophecy is not stated, but the same time period as those against the seacoast is implied by the

---

[1]The prophecy of the people of Judah occupying the seacoasts does not state to what extent they will occupy it. Today the Gaza Strip that occupies much of the area described is part of the Palestinian territory occupied by the modern nation of Israel, and much trouble is brewing. Nor does prophecy always indicate that what will happen is the Lord's will. It merely states that it will happen. This specific prophecy does say the Lord will visit them (Judah) and turn away their captivity (Zephaniah 1:7).

112

reference to the residue of the people of Judah who were to be gathered before the great day of the Lord.

The Lord through Zephaniah then proclaims the fate of the Ethiopians and Assyrians, specifically singling out the ancient city of Nineveh, capital of Assyria. Ethiopia was to be slain by the sword and Assyria destroyed (Zephaniah 2:12–15).

Following his messages of doom to the nations surrounding Judah, the Lord turns to Judah in a similar manner as he did to Israel through the prophet Amos (Amos 1:3–2:5). He describes her rejection of the Lord through following corrupt princes and judges, treacherous prophets, and priests who polluted the sanctuary (temple) and did violence to the law of Moses[2] (Zephaniah 3:1–4). The Lord is just and punished other nations for their iniquity; Judah should have learned from that and received instruction from the Lord, but she also corrupted herself (Zephaniah 3:5–7; compare Jeremiah 3:7–10). The time of Judah's corruption is not specified but is probably a general description of her whole history since the rest of the chapter speaks of the last days. Although Judah had gathered, she had not accepted the gospel.

The book of Zephaniah concludes, as do most of the other Old Testament prophets, with a message of hope. The doom of Judah and surrounding nations had been sounded. The hope is far into the future, in the latter days. There are six parts to this prophetic hope. The Lord will gather all the nations and kingdoms of the world against Judah to pour out his indignation upon them, even to being devoured by his fire (Zephaniah 3:8). This seems to be the same prophecy as Joel's prophecy of all nations gathering into the valley of Jehoshaphat or the valley of decision (Joel 3).

The second part of Zephaniah's prophecy will then be fulfilled— the Lord will restore unto his gathered people a pure language (Zephaniah 3:9). This was interpreted by the Prophet Joseph Smith as the time of the gathering and restoration of Israel, "when he will

---

[2]Violence to the law of Moses probably has reference to the multiplication of interpretation by the elders and rabbis through the years, having lost the true meaning of the law as a schoolmaster to bring them to Christ (Galatians 3:24).

turn to them a pure language, and the earth will be filled with sacred knowledge" (TPJS, p. 93). This language will probably be that of Adam or the language as it was before the Lord confounded the language of all the earth at the time of the building of the tower of Babel (Genesis 11:1–9; see also Moses 6:5–6). The return of this language will better enable the Lord's people to call upon him and serve him with one consent (Zephaniah 1:9). To serve with one consent is probably the law of common consent, the receiving of revelation from the Lord and sustaining the revelation by the voice of the people (D&C 26:2).

Zephaniah's third point is that the Lord's suppliants (messengers) will come from beyond the rivers of Ethiopia to bring the Lord's offering (the gospel). These messengers would be the daughter of Israel's dispersed, the descendants of Israel who had been scattered among the Gentiles but were previously gathered out and the gospel restored to them (Zephaniah 3:10). "Beyond the rivers of Ethiopia" therefore refers to the Americas. This is the same prophecy as given by Isaiah previously (Isaiah 18). The Lord establishes his word in the mouth of two or more witnesses (Deuteronomy 19:15).

In the day that the messengers come to Judah, Judah was to not be ashamed for her transgressions against the Lord and was to lose her pride and haughtiness. This condition was to be brought about because of the holy mountain or temple that would be built among the people of Judah (Zephaniah 3:11). Joseph Smith taught that Judah must return and the temple be rebuilt before the Son of Man would make his appearance (TPJS, pp. 286–87). Thus, to interpret Zephaniah in this manner would sustain the prophecy of Joseph Smith. Those people who are left following the deliverance of Judah from the gentile nations would trust in the Lord even though they were an afflicted and poor people (Zephaniah 3:12). They would also be an honest and fearless people (Zephaniah 3:13). This people would then be as the Book of Mormon teaches, a city built up as a holy city whose inhabitants have been washed in the blood of the Lamb and are partakers of the fulfilling of the covenant that God made to their father Abraham (Ether 13:5, 11).

Old Testament prophecies often refer to more than one people or group. Jacob, son of Lehi, said that "Isaiah spake concerning all the house of Israel" (2 Nephi 6:5). As an example, Jesus quoted Isaiah 52:8–10 as being fulfilled through the latter-day Lamanites. Later he quoted the same verses as being fulfilled through the latter-day Jews.

Therefore, Zephaniah's prophecy may also refer to the people from whom these messengers would come. In the day when these messengers were sent, the people from whom they came — the gathered remnants of Israel in the land of Joseph (the Americas)[3] — will be stripped of their pride and haughtiness. This will be "because" of the Lord's holy mountain (Zephaniah 3:11). The holy mountain may have reference to the temples that will be established among them (Isaiah 2:2–3) or may have a broader interpretation of being "in" the Lord's holy mountain.[4] This latter interpretation would suggest the holy mountain to be the land of America. It would have the same connotation as Jacob's blessing to Joseph concerning a branch of his people extending to the utmost bounds of the everlasting hills, the Americas (Genesis 49:22–26; compare Deuteronomy 33:13–17). This remnant of Israel, although an afflicted and poor people, will trust in the name of the Lord. They will not speak lies nor do iniquity (Zephaniah 3:12–13). The "poor and afflicted people" probably refers to their being persecuted and driven across the United States to settle in the Rocky Mountains.

The daughter of Zion (the remnant in America)[5] is invited by the Lord to sing and to shout. Jerusalem is invited to be glad and rejoice (Zephaniah 3:14). They are to do so because the Lord has cast out their enemy, and he is in the midst of them (Zephaniah

---

[3]The Father covenanted to give the Americas to Joseph's descendants as declared by the Savior to the Nephites when he ministered to them (3 Nephi 15:12–13). This covenant was part of the covenant made with Jacob, father of the twelve tribes (3 Nephi 20:22; Genesis 49:22–26).

[4]The footnote in the LDS edition of the King James Version of the Bible gives "in" as the meaning of the Hebrew word.

[5]The Prophet Joseph Smith identified the Zion spoken of by the Old Testament prophets as North and South America (*TPJS*, p. 362).

3:15). The two nations, originally Israel in the North and Judah in the South, are united again, and one king, the Lord Jesus Christ, will be over them. Jerusalem is not to fear, and Zion is not to slacken her efforts. The Lord will save them and rejoice over them (Zephaniah 3:16–17). Ezekiel foretold the same restoration (Ezekiel 37:15–28).

The last of the six points of Zephaniah's conclusion is regarding the gathering of all the people of Israel and establishing them as a great people in the eyes of all the earth (Zephaniah 3:18–20). Those gathered will be "of thee" (Israel), who have been under the burden of the Gentiles. Those who were driven out will be gathered, and whereas they have been put to shame previously, they will now be praised and become famous. Again Isaiah had foretold the same destiny of scattered Israel when they were gathered (Isaiah 49:7, 23). All of these blessings were to follow Judah's going into captivity.

The book of Zephaniah describes the fall of Jerusalem and the scattering of Judah among the nations. It further describes the eventual gathering of the people of Judah in the last days and a restoration of their blessings as a tribe of the house of Israel. Jesus Christ will become their Lord, their promised Messiah, and their king as they accept and believe in him. They will build a temple and become a Zion people and a holy city. Joseph Smith did not make any changes in the text of Zephaniah as he translated the Bible. Perhaps he did not have time to adequately examine the book. Perhaps it was because most of what Zephaniah prophesied was also foretold by other prophets, but there are important messages within the pages of his record. With Jeremiah he stood as a witness to the nation of Judah and the people of Jerusalem.

Haggai: The Prophet of the Second Temple

The whole purpose of the gathering of the Jews or of any of the house of Israel at any time is to build a temple unto the Lord so that he may reveal his sacred and saving ordinances to his people (*TPJS*, 307–8). Haggai's prophecies illustrate how the Lord works to bring about that purpose.

The Jewish people had gone into Babylon as captives in 607 B.C. (traditional dating). As Jeremiah prophesied, this captivity was to be for seventy years (Jeremiah 25:8–11). At the end of the seventy years (538 B.C. traditional dating), the Lord raised up Cyrus, king of Media and Persia, and inspired him to allow the Jews to return out of captivity to Jerusalem, as prophesied by Isaiah (Isaiah 44:28–45:4; Ezra 1:1–4). Many of the Jews were content in Babylon or did not want to return to Jerusalem. Those Jews who returned found opposition to their rebuilding of the temple from the surrounding inhabitants of the land, the Samaritans (Ezra 4). During the reign of Darius, third king following Cyrus, another group of Jews returned, and the Lord raised up two prophets to inspire the men of Judah to go forward with their work on the rebuilding of the temple. The two prophets were Haggai and Zechariah (Ezra 5:1–2; 6:14). The books of Ezra and Nehemiah give further details of the historical setting for Haggai. The revelations to Haggai as now recorded in the Bible came in the second year of the reign of Darius, two months

117

before the first recorded revelation to Zechariah (Haggai 1:1; Zechariah 1:1). The traditional date of these two writings is 520 B.C. There are four prophecies in the book of Haggai, all of which deal with the time period for rebuilding the temple.

The people in Haggai's day were excusing their inaction by rationalizing that it was not yet time to build the temple (Haggai 1:2). Haggai's first prophecy was in response to this rationalization. "Is it time for you, O ye, to dwell in your ceiled houses and this house [the temple or the Lord's house] lie waste?" (Haggai 1:4). Although they were not building the Lord's house, they were apparently not sparing any efforts to build their own houses. The Lord then reminds them that their unprosperous conditions are the result of their failure to build the temple. Their food, drink, clothing, and wages are all lacking (Haggai 1:5–6). He then invites them to consider their ways and conditions and to know that the drought they are experiencing is due to his withholding the dew from the earth (Haggai 1:7–11). When people do not respond to the Lord's commandments, the Lord has no obligation to bless them (D&C 82:10). In an attempt to teach them the importance of keeping his commandments, he visits them with afflictions, famine, and pestilence (Helaman 12:3). Haggai's message was effective: Zerubbabel, the governor; Joshua, the high priest; and the remnant of the people of Judah who had returned were stirred up by the prophets of the Lord and commenced working once more on the temple (Haggai 1:12–15).

About a month later, the Lord gave Haggai a second revelation for the people of Judah. He asked them to remember the glory of the first temple and compare it with what they were presently building. Apparently, their efforts were not producing a very impressive building, for the Lord answered his own question by saying the comparison was as nothing (Haggai 2:1–3). He encouraged them to be strong and to beautify the building and promised that he would be with them if they would respond (Haggai 2:4–5). The Lord then gave them a reason for the house to be beautified. In a little while (in the Lord's time), he would shake the heavens and the earth, the sea, the dry land, and all the nations; and desire of all nations (the Messiah) would then come. When he came, the temple would be filled with glory (Haggai 2:6–7). This is the only specific Messianic prophecy in the book of Haggai. The shaking of the heaven and earth has reference to the catastrophic signs that occurred at the time of Christ's birth (3 Nephi 1:15–21; Luke 2:8–15; Matthew 2:1–2).[1] While the gospel testaments do not record the temple being filled with glory at his birth, it probably was, and these were manifestations given to faithful people (Luke 2:25–38). All the prophets had foretold this glorious birth — because all nations would be blessed by his advent into mortality, "the desire of all nations" would thus come. The beautiful LDS hymn "Come, O Thou King of Kings" was based upon this inspired verse.[2] The Lord then reminds the people that the silver and the gold of the earth are his, that this second temple will be greater than the former, and that there will be peace in the land when it is completed (Haggai 2:8–9). The Lord would furnish the gold and silver if the people would do their part. This was a great promise: consider that Solomon's building of the first temple was famous among all nations for its beauty! Unfortunately, the Bible does not record the fulfillment of the superior beauty of the second temple; therefore, we do not know if this challenge was met. Someday fuller records may reveal that information.

In another two months, the prophet Haggai received another revelation (Haggai 2:10). Apparently the people lacked righteousness. The Lord through Haggai asked several questions regarding a person's cleanliness under the law of Moses, and the priests responded. Based upon the priest's response, Haggai pronounced that this people and this nation were unclean before the Lord (Haggai 2:11–14). An unclean people cannot build a temple that is holy in the Lord's eyes. The Lord then promised that he

---

[1]Paul quoted Haggai 2:6 as a Second Coming occurrence. Therefore, it seems to be a dual prophecy.

[2]*Hymns*, no. 59.

119

would bless the people from that day forward if they would cleanse themselves and follow him (Haggai 2:15–19). Latter-day revelation teaches that all blessings are predicated upon righteousness (D&C 130:20–21). The people apparently responded to the Lord's promise because they completed the temple.

On the same day that Haggai's third recorded prophecy was given, the Lord revealed the last recorded instructions (Haggai 2:20). This revelation was addressed to the governor Zerubbabel. The Lord told Haggai to tell him not to worry about the threats of surrounding nations and kings because the Lord would overthrow the throne of the heathen kingdoms and destroy their strength. He further promised to make him as a signet, a ring showing that one has authority, because the Lord had chosen him (Haggai 2:21–23). This promise exemplifies the adage that two people can do anything if one of them is the Lord. This promise may also have Messianic overtones—as Zerubbabel appears in the genealogy of Christ, who was the real governor of Judah (Matthew 1:12–13; Luke 3:27).

No more is known about the prophet Haggai. His mission was fruitful. Through him, the Jews who had returned from Babylon were motivated to work on the temple. The temple was completed a few years hence (516 B.C., traditional date). Many faithful people received the sacred blessings of the temple because of Haggai's faith and diligence. He probably had many other revelations, but these four regarding the temple are all that are recorded. They serve as a motivation to the Latter-day Saints who are, as the Lord's covenant people always are, a temple-building people.

Zechariah: Prophet of the Latter-day Judah

The prophet Zechariah was raised up as a second witness to accompany Haggai in encouraging the Jews to rebuild the temple in Jerusalem about 520 B.C. Compared to Haggai's first witness, Zechariah's writings are extensive and cover subjects beyond the building of the temple. In fact, the primary subject of his message is Jesus Christ. His prophecies about Christ relate to both his ministry in the meridian of time and his second coming. The Jews' confusion over these two periods was probably a major reason for many of them rejecting Jesus as the Christ. Jacob, brother of Nephi, said: "But behold, the Jews were a stiffnecked people; and they despised the words of plainness, and killed the prophets, and sought for things that they could not understand. Wherefore, because of their blindness, which blindness came by looking beyond the mark, they must needs fall; for God hath taken away his plainness from them, and delivered unto them many things which they cannot understand, because they desired it. And because they desired it God hath done it, that they may stumble" (Jacob 4:14).

The book of Zechariah is readily separated into two divisions. The first eight chapters cover the return of the Jews to Jerusalem from Babylon and their rebuilding of the city and the temple. Although there are allusions to future events, the basic message is about Zechariah's time. The last six chapters (9–14) are prophecies of both appearances of Jesus Christ — his ministry in the flesh and his coming in glory in the last days.

Zechariah's first two prophecies come in the second year of Darius (Zechariah 1:1, 7). His first was recorded in the middle of Haggai's four prophecies; his second, two months after Haggai's last prophecy. His next prophecy is dated in the fourth year of Darius, two years later than Haggai's last recorded prophecy (Zechariah 7:1). The rest of his prophecies are not dated. Bible scholars do not agree whether Zechariah was the author of the last six chapters or even which Zechariah of the many mentioned in the Bible is the author. I accept Zechariah as the author of the whole book and will not analyze in this work the authorship problems or questions. There is a seeming contradiction between the superscription, which states that Zechariah is the son of Berechiah (Zechariah 1:1), the son of Iddo, and Ezra 5:1 and 6:14, which states that he is the son of Iddo. Some scholars believe that Zechariah was the grandson of Iddo and that Ezra merely skips the father in his genealogy. This is the position I will assume in this work since it has no effect upon the message.

Some believe that this Zechariah was the person Jesus referred to as being slain between the temple and the altar and whose blood would be upon the generation of the Jews (Matthew 23:35). However, the Prophet Joseph Smith identified the slain Zacharias as the father of John the Baptist (TPJS, p. 261). Again, the arguments on this issue will not be considered in this work.

The Rebuilding of the Temple

Zechariah begins his writing with a call to repentance to his Jewish brothers and a reminder that the warnings of the former prophets to their fathers had been fulfilled (Zechariah 1:2–6). There is no mention of the building of the temple in this warning but it is obviously connected with it because, three months later, the Lord gave Zechariah a series of eight visions, all of which are related to the building of the temple. The Lord also gave him the interpretation of these visions, at least in part. This reminds us of a point of doctrine taught by the Prophet Joseph Smith. In speaking of the prophecies of Daniel, he said: "I make this broad declaration, that whenever God gives a vision of an image, or beast, or figure of any kind, He always holds Himself responsible to give a revelation or interpretation of the meaning thereof, otherwise we are not responsible or accountable for our belief in it. Don't be afraid of being damned for not knowing the meaning of a vision or figure, if God has not given a revelation or interpretation of the subject" (*TPJS*, p. 291).

The Prophet's declaration must also apply to Zechariah; therefore I will concentrate on those things revealed to Zechariah and given through other scriptures but will not speculate on other interpretations unless clearly labeled as an opinion.

The first vision that Zechariah saw was of a man riding on a red horse among the myrtle trees, with other horses behind him (Zechariah 1:8). Although the text does not say that men were riding the other horses, it implies that they were. An angel gave Zechariah the meaning of the dream. These men had been sent to the earth by the Lord (Zechariah 1:9–11). Although the angel does not state their mission, from the conversation that follows between the angel and the Lord they appear to be angelic watchmen that the Lord had set upon the city of Jerusalem (see Isaiah 62:6). The angel inquired of the Lord regarding the seventy years of Judah's captivity and was told good and comfortable words. The Lord was jealous for Jerusalem and displeased with the heathen; therefore the Lord would return to Jerusalem and build his house (Zechariah 1:12–16). The Lord's displeasure with the heathen was probably because they had rejected their opportunity to hear the gospel from the Jewish captives. The Lord had a dual purpose in grafting this natural branch of Israel in another part of his vineyard (Jacob 5:8, 14): he was going to preserve that branch for grafting it back in the future, and also he would give the heathen in that area of his vineyard an invitation to be numbered with the house of Israel. While these overall truths were shown or told to Zechariah, the main message was that the Lord desired to build the temple and Zechariah was called to assist in that endeavor. As an afterthought or reminder, the Lord declared that "my cities through prosperity shall yet be spread abroad; and the Lord shall yet comfort Zion, and shall yet choose Jerusalem" (Zechariah 1:17). This was not to be the last gathering to Jerusalem. They would once more be settled among the nations, but in the final outcome there would be two gathering places for the house of Israel—Zion and Jerusalem (2 Nephi 15:10–19). This is also a prevalent theme of the prophet Isaiah (for example, see Isaiah 40:9; 52:1–2).

The second vision shown to Zechariah was of four horns and four carpenters. The four horns were interpreted by the angel to be those who had scattered Judah, Israel, and Jerusalem. The four carpenters were to come and cast out the Gentile who had come to scatter Judah (Zechariah 1:18–21). Whether the four horns were four nations of the past history or four present-day forces upon Judah is not stated, but the latter is more likely. In any case, they represent the Gentile influence among them. The four carpenters might well be the four representatives raised up by the Lord to rebuild his city and his temple. These four would probably be Zerubbabel, the governor; Joshua, the high priest; and the two prophets, Haggai and Zechariah (Ezra 5:1–2). The Lord was once more assuring Zechariah that he was on the Lord's errand.

The third vision, constituting the entire second chapter of Zechariah, is of a man with a measuring line measuring Jerusalem. The man is apparently determining the size of the city. The angel sends another angel to tell the man with the measuring line that Jerusalem shall be inhabited again with many more people and the Lord will be in her midst (Zechariah 2:1–5). The Lord then invites those he has scattered, and particularly those in Babylon, to return and promises to dwell in their midst in Jerusalem (Zechariah 2:6–12). The future of Jerusalem is thus shown to Zechariah.

Zechariah's fourth vision is of Joshua, the high priest, and Satan before the angel. Joshua is clothed in filthy garments, and Satan is there at Joshua's right hand to resist him. The Lord rebukes Satan for his efforts and clothes Joshua in clean garments (Zechariah 3:1–5). Satan's presence is one of the few such occurrences presently

124

recorded in the Old Testament. (He shows up in Job 1 and 2 and in 1 Chronicles 21.) There were probably many other references originally, but they were among the loss of plain and precious truths from the Bible (1 Nephi 13:23–29). Satan, who was responsible for those losses (1 Nephi 13:6, 26), would like us to believe that there is no hell and no devil (2 Nephi 28:22). His reality and his resistance to the Lord's work were shown to Zechariah and may be compared to Moses or Joseph Smith being made aware of Satan's opposition (Moses 1:12–23; JS – H 1:15–16, 20ff). Zechariah was also made aware that Joshua had been cleansed of his sins and was the Lord's anointed servant.

Although Joshua was called by the Lord, the angel admonishes him that he must still meet certain conditions for his eternal salvation and his presence with the heavenly beings (Zechariah 3:6–7). Thus Joshua has his agency to meet or reject these conditions. One's agency is an eternal principle that must always be considered. The angel then seems to speak by divine investiture of authority for the Father, declaring that his servant "the BRANCH" will be brought forth (Zechariah 3:8). The capitalization of the servant's name implies that it is a messianic prophecy. The prophet Jeremiah also identifies the servant as "the BRANCH" (Jeremiah 23:5–6; 33:15). The angel next calls attention to a stone with seven eyes that was laid before Joshua. The interpretation of this stone is not given except that in the Joseph Smith Translation, the Prophet changed references to the seven eyes in later chapters to seven "servants." This reference would probably also have been changed had the Prophet completed his translation work. However, the identity of those seven servants and their mission and time period has not been revealed. They do appear to be angelic beings working upon the earth but beyond the veil. Their work is implied to be in the future because the next comment of the angel, still speaking by divine investiture, is that "I will remove the iniquity of that land in one day" (Zechariah 3:9). This undoubtedly has reference to the Second Coming and is further supported by the following verse's description of all people being neighbors, a millennial concept (Zechariah 3:10).

125

The fifth vision shown to Zechariah is a little more complicated than the previous four. He sees a golden candlestick with a bowl upon the top of it and seven lamps with seven pipes to the lamps on top of the bowl. There are two olive trees by the configuration, one on the right side and one on the left (Zechariah 4:1–3). The interpretation given by the angel is that Zerubbabel has laid the foundation of the temple and will finish it. However, it will not be by his might nor his power but by the Lord's spirit. The seven eyes or servants that ran through the whole earth will apparently provide that spiritual power or at least assist in it. Therefore, the candlestick may represent either the Lord himself or perhaps Zerubbabel, and the bowl represents the temple to be built. The seven lamps are the seven angelic servants who receive their power (pipes) from the Lord.

The angel also answers Zechariah's question about the two olive trees by the structure. They are further described as having two golden pipes that enable them to empty oil out of themselves. The angel identifies these olive trees as "the two anointed ones, that stand *before* the Lord of the whole earth" (JST, Zechariah 4:14; italics added). Thus these olive trees represent the two prophets whom the Lord has raised up to assist Zerubbabel in building the temple. They are Haggai and Zechariah. They are also symbolic of the two prophets who will be raised up in the last days to assist the people of Judah in their battle against the Gentile nations (the battle of Armageddon) (Isaiah 51:18–20; Revelation 11:3–12; D&C 77:15). Remember that all things have their likeness and bear record of Christ (Moses 6:63).

Zechariah's sixth vision was of a flying roll whose length was twenty cubits and whose breadth was ten cubits. The angel interpreted it as a curse that was going over the face of the whole earth. Those guilty of stealing or of swearing were particularly singled out (Zechariah 5:1–4). Nothing else was stated regarding the curse. Perhaps it was symbolic of the apostasy between the time of Malachi, the last prophet, and the coming of Christ. If it was the apostasy, the specific cutting off might represent the loss of the blessings of the prophets, Malachi being the last.

The next vision, the seventh, was of an ephah, a woman in the midst of the ephah, and a talent of lead on the balance scale. The angel interpreted this as wickedness. Two women then lifted up the ephah between the earth and heaven and took it to the land of Shinar (Zechariah 5:6–11). Again no further interpretation is given. If the curse in the fifth vision was the apostasy, perhaps the ephah of wickedness represented the cause of the apostasy.

The last of the eight visions was of four chariots coming out between two mountains of brass. Each of the chariots was drawn by a different color of horse—red, black, white, and grisled and bay (Zechariah 6:1–3). According to the angel, the chariots represented "the four servants of the heavens which go forth from standing before the Lord of all the earth" (JST, Zechariah 6:5). The black horses went into the north and were followed by the white horses. This quieted the Lord's Spirit in the north country. There is no mention of the red horses unless they are "the bay" referred to in the following verse, but the grisled horses went into the south country. The bay horses walked to and fro through the earth, but no effect of their walking is recorded in the text. The following verses seem to be a part of this vision; if they are, the servant's travels probably represent the gathering of the Jews from the various parts of the earth (Zechariah 6:9–10).

Zechariah is instructed to take silver and gold and make crowns, one for the head of Joshua the high priest (Zechariah 6:11). This crowning apparently symbolized Christ as the King of kings, the BRANCH (Zechariah 6:12–13). The text seems to represent both Joshua as the present-day high priest who shall be the presiding authority in the temple, and Jesus Christ, who shall sit upon the throne of David forever (compare 2 Samuel 7:16). The other crowns were for four others who have returned from captivity as a memorial for the temple of the Lord. These were to come and help build the temple (Zechariah 7:14–15). The message to Zechariah is that the temple will be built and Joshua will serve, which is symbolic of

Christ reigning through eternity. Through this series of eight visions, the Lord makes plain to Zechariah that the temple will be built. He also outlines the roles of the various individuals in its building.

The next recorded revelation to Zechariah is given two years later but still seems to be on the subject of the Jews returning and building the temple. While in their seventy-year captivity, apparently the Jews had fasted every fifth month for deliverance. There was now a delegation sent to the priests to see if this practice was to continue. In response, the Lord reminded them that they did not fast unto him nor eat unto him in those seventy years but rather did so unto themselves. Nor had they hearkened to the prophets among them (Zechariah 7:1–7). The Lord reminded them that Zechariah had instructed them to "execute true judgment, and show mercy and compassions every man to his brother; and to oppress not the widow, nor the fatherless, the stranger, nor the poor; and let none of you imagine evil against his brother in your heart" (Zechariah 7:9–10). These instructions are comparable to the definition of true religion given in the New Testament by James (James 1:26–27). The Jews in captivity had not hearkened to these admonitions of the former prophets, so the Lord had scattered them as a whirlwind and left the land desolate (Zechariah 7:11–14). The Lord was warning them to not follow the pattern of their fathers while in captivity.

Following this gentle reminder, the Lord held out a message of hope to his returnees. He promised to dwell in the midst of Jerusalem; the city should be called a city of trust, and the mountain of the Lord of hosts should be called the holy mountain (Zechariah 8:1–3). This may be a promise of his holy temple being in their midst. He further proclaimed that there shall yet be old men and old women dwelling in the streets of Jerusalem as well as boys and girls (Zechariah 8:4–5). These verses are still used as a theme for the present-day returning Jews. Although it was an incentive for the people of Zechariah's day, it may well have been meant as a prophecy intended for the latter days as well. The prophecy continues with a promise to gather the people from the east and the west to Jerusalem, where they would be the Lord's people and he would be their God in truth and righteousness (JST, Zechariah 8:7–8). The Lord then admonished them to hearken to the prophets' words that were given when they laid the foundation of the temple. He promised them that they would prosper and that they would no longer be a curse among the heathen; rather, he would gather both the house of Jacob and Israel, and they would be a blessing (JST, Zechariah 8:9–13). He again reminded them of their duties to be a religious people as outlined by Zechariah previously (Zechariah 8:16–17; compare 7:9–10). The Lord next answered the original question. The fast of the fifth, seventh, and tenth months should be fasts of joy and gladness (Zechariah 8:18–29; compare D&C 59:13–15). The Lord again prophesied that many would return from many cities and many languages because they had heard that God was with the Jews (Zechariah 8:20–23). The Jews did return, although they were scattered again. Today they are experiencing a similar return. Once more, this may have been a dual prophecy.

The Messiah Ministers on Earth

As stated earlier, the book of Zechariah is easily divided into two sections. The second section begins with chapter 9 and introduces a new time period. The first eight verses speak of the burden or message of doom against the various nations surrounding Judah. This message of doom probably refers to the time period from Zechariah's prophecies regarding the rebuilding of the temple around 520 B.C. to the birth of the Messiah. It acts as a buffer between the two time periods spoken of in the first eight chapters and the chapters following.

Following the message of doom in chapter 9, there are three prophecies about the ministry of Christ. Jesus' riding of a colt into the city at the beginning of the last week of his ministry was foretold by Zechariah. Jerusalem was to shout because "thy King cometh to thee: he is just and having salvation; lowly and riding upon an ass, and upon a colt, the foal of an ass" (Zechariah 9:9). As he rode down from Bethphage on the Mount of Olives, the people laid their garments in his path or cut palm branches and laid them before him, proclaiming that he was the Son of David, King of Israel. Both Matthew and John quote Zechariah as being fulfilled with this incident (Matthew 21:1–9; John 12:12–15). The Christian world today celebrates Palm Sunday commemorating this event.

The second prophecy is about the chariot of Ephraim and the horse from Jerusalem being cut off. The King was to speak peace to the heathen, and his dominion was to extend to the ends of the earth (Zechariah 9:10). This prophecy was another way of foretelling that the gospel would be taken from the Jews to the Gentiles. Jesus proclaimed this concept during his ministry (Matthew 19:30; 21:43), and it was fulfilled when Peter received the revelation to take the gospel to the Gentiles (Acts 10). Christ's dominion going to the ends of the earth was in fulfillment of the covenant made to Abraham to bless all nations of the earth (Abraham 2:11; 1 Nephi 22:9; 3 Nephi 20:25).

The third prophecy of Christ's ministry was his opening of the spirit world to the preaching of the gospel and the performing of ordinances for those spirits in prison. Through the blood of his covenant, Christ visited the spirit world and organized the forces of righteous departed spirits to preach the gospel to those in spirit prison and perform the ordinances to bring the "prisoners out of the pit wherein is no water" (Zechariah 9:11; compare D&C 138:18–30). The lack of water is reminiscent of the parable of Lazarus and the rich man taught by Jesus during his ministry. The rich man desired that Lazarus dip his finger in water and cool the rich man's tongue, but the gulf between them made that impossible (Luke 16:19–31). The lack of water probably represents the absence of the living water of Christ and his gospel among the wicked. Christ had not yet bridged the gulf that enabled the gospel to be taught. The rest of the verses in the chapter are addressed to the "prisoners of hope" and seem to be an invitation for those in the spirit prison to accept the gospel: "The Lord their God shall save them in that day" when they shall receive the gospel and be exalted (Zechariah 9:12–17).

In chapter 10 the Lord reflects upon his covenant with Judah and how he will bless the Gentiles when Judah breaks that covenant. He is willing to bless his people (give them rain), but their leaders have pursued vanity and false dreams and left the people without guidance. The Lord was angry with the shepherds (leaders), and the goats (people) were punished. The cornerstone (RSV Christ) came out of Judah, and the political leadership through others; but they shall be overcome by mighty men (the Romans) because the Lord will be with them (Zechariah 10:1–5). The Lord will punish the wicked with the wicked (Mormon 4:5). Although Judah will be overcome, she will be strengthened or gathered again. The Lord will also save and gather the house of Joseph, making them as though they had never been cast off (scattered). Although they were sown among the people (scattered), he shall gather them from the various countries and make them strong in the Lord (Zechariah 10:6–12). Perhaps the Lord turns to Joseph (Ephraim) as his subject because it is through him that Judah will be blessed.

The Lord returns to prophesy of the howling of the shepherds of Judah who will be delivered into their neighbor's hands (Zechariah 11:1–7). Because the rulers of Judah really did know that Jesus was the Christ and yet made a covenant with hell (see Isaiah 28:14–15; compare John 7:26), the Lord let the Romans destroy them. He then comments on the whole house of Israel again. He speaks of his two staves or nations of divided Israel (Judah and Ephraim). Calling northern Israel "Beauty," he speaks of feeding his flock, but they also were led by false shepherds. He speaks of cutting off three shepherds in one month (three kings of Israel, two of whom ruled for only a short period because of their wickedness, probably Jeroboam II, Zechariah, and Shallum, and the one month was really one year — 2 Kings 15:8–15). The Lord refused to feed his people in their wickedness and cut Beauty asunder. He broke his covenant with Northern Israel, which the people knew was the Lord's doing as they were taken captive by Assyria in 721 B.C. (Zechariah 11:7–11).

The prophecy once more shifts to Judah and the Lord's breaking of the covenant with them. He foretells that Judas would betray the Christ for thirty pieces of silver and cast the money into the potter's field (Zechariah 11:12–13). Credit for this prophecy is given to Jeremiah in the New Testament (Matthew 27:1–10). Perhaps Jeremiah made the same or a similar prophecy; regardless, it was fulfilled by Judas. The other stave or nation of Judah called "Bands" was also cut asunder, and the brotherhood between Judah and Israel was broken (Zechariah 11:14).

The Lord through Zechariah follows this prophecy with a prophecy of how he will cut Judah asunder. A foolish shepherd will be raised up who will have no concern for his sheep (Judah). He will not care for his lambs (Zechariah 11:15–16). This prophecy may refer to the conquest by Rome or to the ruler Constantine and others. Constantine adopted Christianity as his state religion but brought about the apostasy through not shepherding the flock. The Lord utters a warning to this foolish shepherd who leaves his flock (RSV, Zechariah 11:17). This suggests Constantine, who brought pagans into the fold instead of the Lord's people. The fate of his arm being dried up and his eye darkened may also suggest Constantine, who would lose his power and darken the gospel message. The times of the Gentiles was there, and Israel was delegated to receive the gospel again after the Gentiles had rejected it in the latter days. The first shall be last and the last shall be first (see Matthew 19:30).

The Messiah's Second Coming

The last three chapters may be yet a third distinct section of the text of Zechariah. These chapters refer to still a third time period — the coming of the Lord in the last days or his second coming. The chronology given is not consistent with itself or with latter-day scripture, but the teachings are confirmed by modern revelation.

A burden or message of doom to Israel opens this last section of Zechariah. The Lord promises to make Jerusalem a cup of trembling unto all the people round about when they lay siege against Judah and Jerusalem. All of the people of the earth will be gathered against Jerusalem. The governors or leaders of Judah are to devour the people round about, and the Lord will defend Jerusalem (Zechariah 12:1–8). This is another description of the Battle of Armageddon (Revelation 16:16) or the valley of decision (Joel 3). At the conclusion of the battle, the Lord will appear to his people, the embattled Jews; they will recognize him as their messiah and "will look upon me whom they have pierced" (Zechariah 12:10). There is a dual fulfillment or application of this prophecy. It was quoted by John in his gospel as being fulfilled while Christ was on the cross (John 19:37). However, the same author spoke of his coming in the clouds of heaven when "every eye shall see him, and they also which pierced him" (Revelation 1:7). The context of Zechariah supports the latter fulfillment. The text continues with a declaration that there would be great mourning in Jerusalem in that day (Zechariah 12:11–14).

The following chapter also speaks of a day of restoration among Judah. It speaks of a fountain that would be "opened to the house of David and to the inhabitants of Jerusalem for sin and for uncleanness" (Zechariah 13:1). This has reference to the ordinance of baptism for the remission of individual sins and is supported by the prophet Isaiah's declarations of Judah opening the gate of baptism as well as a political invitation to the nation that "keepeth the truth" (see Isaiah 26:2). Thus the gospel will be preached in the Jewish homeland to the Jews.

Zechariah continues with a prophecy of idols and false prophets being cut off in the land (Zechariah 13:2–5). This prophecy must be read in its context carefully to note that it is speaking of false prophets. The text returns to an extension of Zechariah 12:10. As they look upon him whom they have pierced, one shall say to the Savior, "What are these wounds in thine hands?" Then he shall answer, "Those with which I was wounded in the house of my friends" (Zechariah 13:6). The Doctrine and Covenants records these same words as given by Jesus on the Mount of Olives to his disciples prior to his crucifixion regarding the events of the last days. It further equates it with the mourning mentioned in the previous chapter of Zechariah (D&C 45:51–53). The chapter is concluded with a prophecy that two-thirds of the Jewish people will be killed in the battle of Armageddon but the third that survive will be refined and made the people of the Lord (Zechariah 13:7–9).

The final chapter of Zechariah speaks of the coming of the "day of the Lord." It is the day when all nations shall gather against Jerusalem to battle and the Lord will fight against those nations (Zechariah 14:1–3). When the Lord appears, his feet shall stand upon the mount of Olives, and it shall cleave in the midst toward the east and the west with the mount being moved half to the north and half to the south (Zechariah 14:4). The Lord also referred to this catastrophic event in the appendix of the Doctrine and Covenants (D&C 133:18–20; see also D&C 45:48). He compared the fleeing of the people at this time to the earthquake in the days of Uzziah (Zechariah 14:5). There is no record of an earthquake in Uzziah's day, but there must have been one. This earthquake is a pattern or type of the earthquake that was to come in the last days (compare Moses 6:63).

Another sign apparently to be repeated is the day and a night and a day of no darkness given to the Nephites at the birth of Christ happening again at the Second Coming (3 Nephi 1:15–19). In Zechariah's words, the light shall not be clear nor light but at evening time it shall be light (Zechariah 14:6–7). The wording of this prophecy is a bit nebulous, but it seems similar to the Nephite sign.

The earthquake was to accompany the coming of the Lord and all the Saints with him (Zechariah 14:5). The Savior's instructions to his disciples on the mount of Olives qualifies the Saints coming with him as the Jewish Saints who have slept or died being resurrected at his coming (D&C 45:43–46). This was to happen before the arm of the Lord fell upon the surrounding nations (D&C 45:45).

Zechariah next speaks of living water coming out from Jerusalem, half toward the former sea (Mediterranean) and half toward the hinder sea (Dead Sea). This water was to run in the winter as well as the summer (Zechariah 14:8). The living water is symbolic of Christ (compare John 4:10–15; 7:37). However, the Prophet Joseph

Smith spoke of the actual water that would come from under the temple that was to be built in Jerusalem (*TPJS*, pp. 286–87; Joel 3:18). Following the above events, the Lord will be king over all the earth, and Jerusalem shall be inhabited safely (Zechariah 14:9–11). The Doctrine and Covenants repeatedly speaks of Jesus' reign as the king (D&C 38:21; 41:4; 45:59; 58:22; 65:5–6). Other Old Testament prophets have also prophesied of his role as king (Jeremiah 23:5; Ezekiel 34:23–24; 37:24–27).

Zechariah next speaks of the plague that will come upon those who fight against Jerusalem. Flesh, eyes, and tongues shall fall away (Zechariah 14:12). This sounds like the same plagues mentioned in D&C 29:18–20 that will come before the great day of the Lord. Zechariah speaks further of those who will not come up to Jerusalem to worship (Zechariah 14:16–19). Although the feast of the tabernacles (a festival under the law of Moses) is mentioned, it is probably symbolic of the higher law that will be followed in the Millennium.

The text concludes with an announcement that even the bells of the horses, as well as pots and other items, will have engraved upon them "Holiness to the Lord." There will be no more Canaanites or Gentiles in the house of the Lord (Zechariah 14:20–21). The Prophet Joseph reaffirmed this as a latter-day practice (*TPJS*, p. 93). It is another way of describing Jerusalem as a holy city unto the Lord, occupied by a holy or sanctified people (Ether 13:5, 11).

The prophet Zechariah was a second witness with Haggai to motivate the rebuilding of the Lord's temple in 520 B.C. He also saw the meridian of time and the mission of the Lord Jesus Christ. His prophecies extended to the final winding-up scenes in Jerusalem and the coming of the great day of the Lord. Just as the Jews looked beyond the mark and confused the prophecies of the Second Coming with those of the first coming, we must carefully study the writings of Zechariah so that we do not confuse the two time periods. Zechariah has left us a challenging text to study, and the Lord has confirmed his prophecies in the Doctrine and Covenants.

Malachi: Prophet of the Everlasting Covenant

The prophecies of Malachi are of great interest to the Latter-day Saints. They speak of things that must happen before the second coming of Christ and of how one must prepare for that great event. They clearly proclaim that the everlasting covenant, or the gospel of Jesus Christ, must be restored upon the earth in preparation for the great and dreadful day of the Lord—great for those who are prepared, and dreadful for those who are not prepared.

The importance and relevance of the last two chapters of the book of Malachi were confirmed on two different occasions. When the Savior visited the Nephites following his resurrection, "he commanded them that they should write the words which the Father had given unto Malachi, which he should tell them" (3 Nephi 24:1). The words that he told them to write were the third and fourth chapters of Malachi as we know them today (3 Nephi 24–25). After they were written, he expanded them, but what he said was not recorded (3 Nephi 26:1).

The second confirming occasion of Malachi's words was the appearance of Moroni to Joseph Smith on the morning of 22 September 1823. The angel "quoted part of the third chapter . . . also the fourth or last chapter of the prophecy, though with a little variation from the way it reads in our Bible" (JS–H 1:36). That the third and fourth chapters were quoted on both occasions is evidence that these two are the most significant of the entire book. This is probably because the first two chapters deal primarily with Malachi's day, while the last two pertain to the restoration of the gospel in the latter days. While the emphasis of this work will be on the last two chapters, the first two do set the stage for the latter ones and need some clarification.

The superscription gives no historical setting, merely labeling Malachi's words as "the burden of the word of the Lord to Israel" (Malachi 1:1). As previously stated, the burden has reference to a message of doom. Its being addressed to Israel and the context of the restoration chapters that follow suggest that the Lord is outlining why the gospel was taken from Israel for a time and given to the Gentiles.

The Lord begins his message by declaring that he has loved Israel, but Israel questions whether he really has. The Lord then responds, "Was not Esau Jacob's brother? . . . yet I loved Jacob. And I hated Esau, and laid his mountains and his heritage waste for the dragons of the wilderness" (Malachi 1:2–3). Some have misinterpreted this passage to reflect that God is a respecter of persons, but Paul answered such accusations in his epistle to the Romans by showing that election in the flesh does not assure salvation (Romans 9:4–18). Brigham Young and Willard Richards shed further light on the issue:

> "As it is written, Jacob have I loved, but Esau have I hated." Where is it written? (Mal. i:1,2). When was it written? About 397 years before Christ, and Esau and Jacob were born about 1,773 years before Christ, (according to the computation of time in Scripture margin), so Esau and Jacob lived about 1,376 years before the Lord spoke by Malachi, saying, "Jacob have I loved, but Esau have I hated," as quoted by Paul. This text is often brought forward to prove that God loved Jacob and hated Esau before they were born, or before they had done good or evil; but if God did love one and hate the other before they had done good or evil, He has not seen fit to tell us of it, either in the Old or New Testament, or any other revelation: but this

137

only we learn that 1,376 years after Esau and Jacob were born, God said by Malachi — "Jacob have I loved, and Esau have I hated;" and surely that was time sufficient to prove their works, and ascertain whether they were worthy to be loved or hated.

And why did He love the one and hate the other? For the same reason that He accepted the offering of Abel and rejected Cain's offering. Because Jacob's works had been righteous, and Esau's wicked, and where is there a righteous father who would not do the same thing? Who would not love an affectionate and obedient son more than one who was disobedient, and sought to injure Him and overthrow the order of His house? (HC 4:262.)

The Lord then affirms that his blessings are upon Israel (Jacob) and not on Edom (Esau) (Malachi 1:4–5).

The Lord's first complaint against Israel is that the people have despised his name by offering polluted and inferior sacrifices. Because of this condition, the Lord said that he would turn from Israel to the Gentiles, and his name would be great among them (Malachi 1:6–14).

The Lord next addresses the priests, threatening a curse upon them if they do not hearken to his words. The Lord had extended his priesthood covenant to the sons of Levi because of their love of truth and dedication to service. By Malachi's day, the priests of Israel had broken that covenant of Levi (Malachi 2:1–10).

The third complaint is against Judah in general. Judah has profaned the holiness of the Lord and married the daughter of a strange God. The wife of Judah's youth has been dealt with treacherously (Malachi 2:11–16). The symbolism used here is unusual compared with the typical marriage symbolism of Christ as the bridegroom and Israel as the bride. This symbolism seems to identify the church as the bride of Judah's youth, as it also does in the book of Revelation (Revelation 12:1–6). Judah has desecrated the church and has been affiliating with the religion (daughter) of a pagan (strange) god.

The Lord then announces that Israel has wearied him with their words. In response to their supposed innocence, he accuses them of justifying the evil that they do as being good in the sight of the Lord because the Lord has not brought judgment against them (Malachi 2:17). This is similar to Noah's day when the people claimed that God could not be angry with them because they were eating and drinking and marrying and giving in marriage and being successful, therefore the Lord could not be displeased with them or he would have punished them (Moses 8:21). The Lord allows mankind their agency and, after warning them by the prophets, brings destruction upon them if they become ripened in iniquity and do not repent (1 Nephi 17:35–38; Genesis 15:16). The people of Noah's day were eventually destroyed. The people of Malachi's day were being warned by the prophets. This succinct announcement concluded the Lord's complaints against the people of Judah in the days of Malachi.

After recognizing the evil conditions that exist in Judah and Jerusalem, the Lord reveals through Malachi how he will correct the situation. The plan disclosed in the last two chapters, quoted to the Nephites and to Joseph Smith, seems to be an explanation of how the Lord's name will be great among the Gentiles. As previously recognized, it will take place before and in preparation for the second coming of the Lord.

The Lord promises to send his messenger to prepare the way before his coming (Malachi 3:1). A surface reading and cross-referencing to the New Testament suggest this to be fulfilled through the mission of John the Baptist (Matthew 11:10; Mark 1:2; Luke 7:27). Although we are dealing with dual prophecy, the ultimate fulfillment will be in the latter days. This is obvious because the Savior quoted this passage to the Nephites following his resurrection and in the context of future fulfillment, and the angel Moroni quoted it among other prophecies soon to be fulfilled; finally, the Savior revealed it again to Joseph Smith in March 1831, this time in the past tense: "And even so I have sent mine everlasting covenant into the world, to be a light to the world, and to be a standard for

139

my people, and for the Gentiles to seek to it, and to be a messenger before my face to prepare the way before me" (D&C 45:9).

The messenger to prepare the way before the second coming of the Lord is therefore the restoration of the everlasting covenant, or the fulness of the gospel. The rest of verse 1 of Malachi 3 further confirms the latter-day fulfillment.

Malachi prophesied that the Lord would come suddenly to his temple (Malachi 3:1). Following the restoration of the new and everlasting covenant, the Lord reaffirmed his future sudden appearance in his temple (D&C 36:4; 132:2). He could not make this appearance until a temple had been built. The first temple was the Kirtland Temple, completed and dedicated on 3 April 1836. The Lord came to the Kirtland Temple suddenly. Following the prayer of Joseph Smith and Oliver Cowdery, the veil was taken from their minds and eyes, and they saw him (D&C 110:1). Through his atoning blood, he had made the covenant to bring mankind to immortality and eternal life (Hebrews 13:20; Moses 1:39). His appearance fulfilled the promise made through Malachi and established that covenant again in preparation for his second coming.

That Malachi's prophecy is about the second coming of Christ and not the Lord's first ministry is further attested to by the declaration, "But who may abide the day of his coming, and who shall stand when he appeareth? For he is like a refiner's fire and like fuller's soap" (Malachi 3:2). There is no evidence that people could not abide his first coming. His second coming, however, will constitute a cleansing of the earth; thus the analogy of a refiner's fire, in which the impurities are cleansed from ores to make metals. In latter-day revelation, the Lord has declared that "every corruptible thing, both of man, or of the beasts of the field, or of the fowls of the heavens, or of the fish of the sea, that dwells upon all the face of the earth, shall be consumed" (D&C 101:24). The fuller's soap of ancient days was also a purifier often used to whiten cloth.

Malachi's prophecy of the purifying of the sons of Levi that they may offer an offering in righteousness (Malachi 3:3) was also a promise given by John the Baptist when the Aaronic Priesthood was restored to Joseph Smith and Oliver Cowdery on 15 May 1829 (D&C 13). This prophecy has a dual fulfillment. First, after Moses descended the mount and found his people worshiping the golden calf, the tribe of Levi was given the responsibility of carrying out the priesthood ordinances for all of the tribes of Israel (Exodus 32:19–29; Numbers 18:1–8). This assignment continued until the ten tribes were taken away and probably after they went into the North. It was also among the people of Judah until their apostasy. When the ten tribes return, as a part of the restoration of all things in the dispensation of the fulness of time (Ephesians 1:10), they will again offer a literal sacrifice in righteousness. The Prophet Joseph Smith explained:

> These sacrifices, as well as every ordinance belonging to the Priesthood, will, when the Temple of the Lord shall be built, and the sons of Levi be purified, be fully restored and attended to in all their powers, ramifications, and blessings. This ever did and ever will exist when the powers of the Melchizedek Priesthood are sufficiently manifest; else how can the restitution of all things spoken of by the Holy Prophets be brought to pass. It is not to be understood that the law of Moses will be established again with all its rites and variety of ceremonies; this has never been spoken of by the prophets; but those things which existed prior to Moses' day, namely, sacrifice, will be continued.
>
> It may be asked by some, what necessity for sacrifice, since the Great Sacrifice was offered? In answer to which, if repentance, baptism, and faith existed prior to the days of Christ, what necessity for them since that time? The Priesthood has descended in a regular line from father to son, through their succeeding generations (*TPJS*, p. 173).

A second fulfillment of this prophecy of Malachi is established through the latter-day temple work for the dead. In an epistle to the Saints upon this subject on 6 September 1842, the Prophet Joseph Smith wrote that the great day of the Lord was at hand and, after quoting Malachi 3:2–3, declared, "Let us therefore as a church and a people, and as Latter-day Saints, offer unto the Lord an offering in righteousness; and let us present in his holy temple, when it is finished, a book containing the records of our dead, which shall be worthy of all acceptation" (D&C 128:24). This spiritual interpretation is probably based upon the fact that genealogical research must be done at the sacrifice of time and personal interests. It is not something that is scheduled in the Church but must be done on our own initiative.

The offering of Judah and Jerusalem is to be pleasant to the Lord at this time (Malachi 3:4). Judah rejected the higher law of Christ and continued in the law of Moses (Isaiah 29:1–2). Therefore, her sacrifices through the years have not been pleasant to the Lord. As the ten tribes return, the Jewish people will already have begun to accept the gospel (Jacob 5:63), and thus the Lord will accept their sacrifices. The judgments of God will come upon the wicked at this time also (Malachi 3:5). Since the Lord is unchanging, he will not consume the sons of Jacob (Malachi 3:6). He has covenanted to gather them, and he will do so.

There are several things of which the modern-day sons of Jacob must repent before their salvation can be obtained. Like their fathers of old, they have strayed. In the typical style of the previous chapters, the Lord through Malachi states the problem, the sons of Jacob ask how they are guilty, and the Lord gives the answer (Malachi 3:7). The first problem is the robbing of God through withholding tithes and offerings (Malachi 3:8). This refers to latter-day sons of Jacob, members of The Church of Jesus Christ of Latter-day Saints. Those of the Church who do not pay tithing will not survive the judgment to come upon the world (D&C 64:23–24). Failure to comply has brought a curse upon the whole nation (Malachi 3:9). The Lord then challenges the sons of Jacob to bring all their tithes to him, not just some of it or by some of the people, and test him to see if he "will not open you the windows of heaven, and pour you out a blessing that there shall not be room enough to receive it" (Malachi 3:10). This oft-quoted scripture has been equated with rain coming upon the crops, becoming rich through tithe paying, and undoubtedly several other blessings. While these are sometimes the fulfillment, the principle involved was taught by President Harold B. Lee in this way: "The promise following obedience to this principle is that the windows of heaven would be open and blessings would be poured out that we would hardly be able to contain. The opening of the windows of heaven, of course, means revelations from God to him who is willing thus to sacrifice" (*Ensign*, November 1971, p. 16).

President Gordon B. Hinckley reminded the Church that the Lord would open the windows of heaven according to their need and not according to their greed (see CR, April 1982).

A second promise to the tithe payer was that the Lord would rebuke the devourer and not cause the fruits to be destroyed or not be productive (Malachi 3:11). This problem relates more to the weather. The elements that destroy crops include such things as frost, drought, insects, and hail. The Lord promises to control such for his people if they are faithful. Such blessings upon the sons of Jacob will bring the recognition of surrounding nations upon them (Malachi 3:12).

A second sin that the latter-day sons of Jacob must repent of is speaking against the Lord. Again the sons say they are not guilty, but the Lord specifies that they say it is vain to serve God (Malachi 3:13–15). How many members of the latter-day Church fail to recognize the Lord's hand in the weather, in spite of many scriptures that proclaim that he does in fact use the weather to chasten or bless his people (Helaman 12:1–3; D&C 43:25; Amos 4:6–10).

Not all the sons of Jacob are guilty of these sins. Those who fear or love the Lord will have their names recorded in the Lord's book of remembrance. These will be the Lord's people in the day that he makes up his jewels; they will be spared the destructive judgment that comes upon the world (Malachi 3:16–18). The Lord confirmed this promise to the Latter-day Saints in December 1833 (D&C 101:3). A jewel reflects light, and the Lord's people will reflect his light as they have been commanded (3 Nephi 18:24). These people will be prepared for the Lord's second coming.

In Malachi 4, the Lord speaks of the day when the proud and

wicked would burn as stubble. In September 1830 the Lord revealed to Joseph Smith that this day (in the Lord's time) was soon at hand (D&C 29:9). The Book of Mormon bears similar testimony (1 Nephi 22:15; 2 Nephi 26:4).[1] The angel Moroni quoted this passage in Malachi a little differently than it is recorded in the Bible or the Book of Mormon. This was probably to clarify its meaning rather than to correct the text. As time passes, the usage and understanding of words and passages change. The two texts are duplicated here to illustrate the differences:

For, behold, the day cometh, that shall burn as an oven; and all the proud, yea, and all that do wickedly, shall be stubble: and the day that cometh shall burn them up saith the Lord of hosts, that it shall leave them neither root nor branch (Malachi 4:1).	For behold, the day cometh that shall burn as an oven, and all the proud, yea, and all that do wickedly shall *burn as* stubble; for *they* that come shall burn them, saith the Lord of Hosts, that it shall leave them neither root not branch" (JS–H 1:37; italics added).

The message is the same, but Moroni stated it more clearly. The wicked shall burn, and those who come under the Lord's direction (destroying angels) shall supervise or cause the burning. Those who escape the burning will be the tithepayers (D&C 64:23–24). Those who are burned will be left without root or branch, or, in the words of Elder Theodore M. Burton: "What is meant by the expression 'that it shall leave them neither root nor branch'? This expression simply means that wicked and indifferent persons who reject the gospel of Jesus Christ will have no family inheritance or patriarchal lineage—neither root (ancestors or progenitors) nor branch (children or posterity). Such persons cannot be received into the celestial kingdom of glory of resurrected beings, but must be content with a lesser blessing" (CR, September 1967, p. 81).

---

[1]The quotations in the Book of Mormon, being drawn from the plates of brass that did not include Malachi, show that other prophets had foretold of this burning and that Malachi was quoting from an earlier source.

The Lord once more holds out hope to those who fear his name. The Son of Righteousness will arise with healing in his wings (Malachi 4:2; 3 Nephi 25:2). The Book of Mormon text changes the word Sun to Son, referring to the Son of God (2 Nephi 25:13; 26:9). Those who are left after the judgment of the Second Coming will be able to raise up their children as calves are raised in a stall. The calf is protected from the elements, and his environment is controlled (Malachi 4:2; 1 Nephi 22:24). The children in the Millennium will similarly "grow up without sin unto salvation" (D&C 45:58). The telestial element will be removed, and with Satan being bound (Revelation 20:1–3; 1 Nephi 22:26; D&C 101:28), the environment will be more controlled. The wicked who are destroyed, the telestial people, will have their ashes walked upon by those who survive the burning (Malachi 4:3).

The law of Moses that was first given in Mount Horeb or Sinai will by this time be restored to the earth (Malachi 4:4). This is sometimes confusing to the reader, as it appears to be a return to the law of Moses. But when we remember that the Lord took away the Melchizedek Priesthood and the higher law, leaving the Aaronic Priesthood and the lesser law of Moses, it makes sense (see D&C 84:25–27; JST, Exodus 34:1–2; JST, Deuteronomy 10:1–2). In support of the fuller law of Moses being restored, Joseph Smith said, "The law revealed to Moses in Horeb never was revealed to the children of Israel as a nation" (*TPJS*, p. 323).

The coming of Elijah before the great and dreadful day of the Lord, an event still looked forward to by the Jewish nation, was the last great doctrine taught by Malachi (Malachi 4:5–6; D&C 138:46–47; D&C 35:4). The angel Moroni also quoted these last two verses differently. Again, the differences were to clarify the meaning. After quoting these two verses in an epistle to the Saints in 1842, precisely as they are in the Book of Mormon and the Bible, Joseph commented: "I might have rendered a plainer translation to this, but it is sufficiently plain to suit my purpose as it stands" (D&C 128:17–18). A comparison of the two texts illustrates the difference:

145

Behold I will send you Elijah the prophet before the coming of the great and dreadful day of the Lord: And he shall turn the heart of the fathers to the children, and the heart of the children to the fathers, lest I come and smite the earth with a curse (Malachi 4:5–6).

Behold, I will *reveal unto you the Priesthood, by the hand of* Elijah the prophet, before the coming of the great and dreadful day of the Lord.

He also quoted the next verse differently: And he shall plant in the hearts of the *children the promises made to* the fathers, and the hearts of the children *shall turn* to their fathers. *If it were not so, the whole* earth *would be utterly wasted at his coming* (JS–H 1:38–39; italics added).

The priesthood that was to be revealed by Elijah was not the Aaronic or the Melchizedek, because they were both restored before Elijah's appearance on 3 April 1836. Insight into the priesthood that Elijah restored can be gained from the Prophet Joseph Smith:

> Elijah was the last Prophet that held the keys of the Priesthood, and who will, before the last dispensation, restore the authority and deliver the keys of the Priesthood, in order that all the ordinances may be attended to in righteousness. It is true that the Savior had authority and power to bestow this blessing: but the sons of Levi were too prejudiced. "And I will send Elijah the Prophet before the great and terrible day of the Lord," etc., etc. Why send Elijah? Because he holds the keys of the authority to administer in all the ordinances of the Priesthood; and without the authority is given, the ordinances could not be administered in righteousness (*TPJS*, p. 172).

Joseph Smith also taught that the whole purpose of the gathering of Israel in any age of the world "was to build unto the Lord a house whereby He could reveal unto His people the ordinances of His house and the glories of His kingdom, and teach the people the way of salvation" (*TPJS*, pp. 307–8). This concept helps explain why

Elijah did not come until the temple in Kirtland, the first in this dispensation, was completed.

Although all priesthood is Melchizedek, Joseph Smith later referred to the three grand orders of the priesthood: the Melchizedek, the Patriarchal, and the Levitical. He instructed the Saints to "go to and finish the temple, and God will fill it with power, and you will then receive more knowledge concerning this priesthood" (*TPJS*, pp. 322–23). The priesthood restored by Elijah, as stated by the angel Moroni, was evidently the patriarchal order of the priesthood, the power to seal the living and the dead as eternal families.

The promises made to the fathers were the promises of the Restoration and the work for the dead. Enos and his fathers were promised that the Book of Mormon would come forth (Enos 1:15–18; D&C 10:46–52). Abraham rejoiced to see the day of the Savior (John 8:56). The founding fathers were given promise of their work being done for them (*JD*, 19:229). The ancestors of the present-day Latter-day Saints were also given promises, and these promises were planted in the Saints' hearts (Malachi 4:6; D&C 2). The keys of the power of turning the hearts of the fathers to the children, and the children to the fathers, were committed to Elijah (D&C 27:9). Joseph Smith said that Elijah would "reveal the covenants of the fathers in relation to the children, and the covenants of the children in relation to the fathers" (*TPJS*, p. 321).

The hearts of the children were to turn to their fathers (Malachi 4:6); that is, the spirit of Elijah was to move upon them. The Saints were admonished to seek diligently to accomplish this command-ment (D&C 98:16–17). Joseph Smith said regarding this:

> Now, the word *turn* here should be translated *bind*, or seal. But what is the object of this important mission? or how is it to be fulfilled? The keys are to be delivered, the spirit of Elijah is to come, the Gospel to be established, the Saints of God gathered, Zion built up, and the Saints to come up as saviors on Mount Zion.
>
> But how are they to become saviors on Mount Zion? By

147

building their temples, erecting their baptismal fonts, and going forth and receiving all the ordinances, baptisms, confirmations, washings, anointings, ordinations and sealing powers upon their heads, in behalf of all their progenitors who are dead, and redeem them that they may come forth in the first resurrection and be exalted to thrones of glory with them; and herein is the chain that binds the hearts of the fathers to the children, and the children to the fathers, which fulfills the mission of Elijah. And I would to God that this temple was now done, that we might go into it, and go to work and improve our time, and make use of the seals while they are on earth (*TPJS*, p. 330).

Joseph also said that God would rescue this generation by sending Elijah the prophet. Elijah would reveal the covenants to seal the hearts of the fathers to the children, and the children to the fathers (*TPJS*, p. 323). After testifying that the signs of the coming of the Son of Man had already commenced, Joseph declared that "the hearts of the children of men will have to be turned to the fathers, and the fathers to the children, living or dead, to prepare them for the coming of the Son of Man. If Elijah did not come, the whole earth would be smitten" (*TPJS*, p. 160). The angel Moroni reworded the ending statement of the book of Malachi to read: "If it were not so, the whole earth would be utterly wasted at his coming" (D&C 2:3). God is a just God, and through the work of Elijah he has provided an opportunity for all to have an opportunity to receive the ordinances for salvation. Anything short of complete justice would result in God being partial, and the earth would not fulfill the purpose of its creation, namely, for his children to possess it and have the opportunity to keep his commandments (1 Nephi 17:36; Jacob 2:21). The curse of the earth was removed when the Lord provided a welding link between the fathers and the children through baptism and other work for the dead (D&C 128:18).

Another statement of the Prophet Joseph is a good summary of the mission of Elijah:

Now for Elijah. The spirit, power, and calling of Elijah

is that ye have power to hold the key of the revelations, ordinances, oracles, powers and endowments of the fulness of the Melchizedek Priesthood and of the kingdom of God on the earth; and to receive, obtain, and perform all the ordinances belonging to the kingdom of God, even unto the children, and the hearts of the children unto the fathers, even those who are in heaven.

Now comes the point. What is this office and work of Elijah? It is one of the greatest and most important subjects that God has revealed. He should send Elijah to seal the children to the fathers, and the fathers to the children (*TPJS*, p. 337).

This summary statement of Joseph's helps us understand why he later said, "The greatest responsibility in this world that God has laid upon us is to seek after our dead" (*TPJS*, p. 356). The prophet Elijah has come; he restored the keys for his work in the Kirtland Temple on 3 April 1836 (D&C 110:14–16). The work that he restored is under way, and the coming of the great and dreadful day of the Lord is much nearer.

Appendix: Cross-References to the Twelve Prophets

Book	JST	Book of Mormon	Doctrine & Covenants	New Testament	General Authorities
Hosea 1:10				Rom. 9:26	
Hosea 2:23				Rom. 9:25	
Hosea 6:2					TPJS 286
Hosea 6:6				Matt. 9:13; 12:7	
Hosea 11:1				Matt. 2:15	
Hosea 11:8	C				
Hosea 13:14		Mos. 16:7–8		1 Cor. 15:55	
Joel 1:6	C				
Joel 2:2					TPJS 141
Joel 2:10–11, 31			29:14; 34:8–9 43:18; 84:118		
Joel 2:13–14	C				
Joel 2:28–32			95:4	Acts 2:16–21	JS—Hist. 1:41; JD 19:168–69
Joel 2:30–31					TPJS 70–71
Joel 2:32				Rom. 10:13	TPJS 17

Book	JST	Book of Mormon	Doctrine & Covenants	New Testament	General Authorities
Joel 3:16			21:6; 35:24		
Amos 3:6–7	C				TPJS 265, 280; LR Oct. 75, p. 73; MEP Apr. 78, p. 95; Oct. 83, p. 43
Amos 4:3	C				
Amos 4:5–6	Insig.				
Amos 5:25–27				Acts 7:42–43	
Amos 6:10	Insig.				
Amos 7:3, 6	C				
Amos 8:11–12					SWK CR Apr. 64; JBW Oct. 75, p. 155
Amos 9:8	C				
Amos 9:8–9					SWK CR Oct. 75
Obadiah 1:1			1:36		
Obadiah 1:21					TPJS 189, 191, 223, 330; JD 21:97; TMB Oct. 70, p. 35
Jonah 1:17				Matt. 12:38–41; 16:1–4	
Jonah 3:9–10	C				
Micah 4:4					MFP 2:32; TPJS p. 93
Micah 4:11–13		3 Ne. 20:18–19	133:59		

Book	JST	Book of Mormon	Doctrine & Covenants	New Testament	General Authorities
Micah 5:2				Matt. 2:6; John 7:42	
Micah 5:8–9		3 Ne. 16:14–15; 3 Ne. 20:16–17			
Micah 5:8–15		3 Ne. 21:12–21	87:5		JFS DS 2:249–51; SWK Oct. 47, p. 22
Micah 7:6				Matt. 11:36; Luke 12:53	
Nahum 1:8	Insig.				
Habakkuk 1:5		3 Ne. 21:5		Acts 13:40–41	
Habakkuk 2:3–4				Rom. 1:17; Gal. 3:11; Heb. 10:38	
Zephaniah 3:9					TPJS 93
Haggai				Heb. 12:26	
Zechariah 4:7					TPJS 163
Zechariah 4:10, 14	C				
Zechariah 6:5, 7, 13	C				
Zechariah 8:7, 13	C				
Zechariah 9:9				Matt. 21:5; John 12:15	
Zechariah 11:13				Matt. 27:9*	
Zechariah 12:10			43:51, 53	John 19:37	

*Attributed to Jeremy

Book	JST	Book of Mormon	Doctrine & Covenants	New Testament	General Authorities
Zechariah 13:6			45:52		
Zechariah 13:7				Matt. 13:7; Mark 14:27	
Zechariah 14:4			133:20		
Zechariah 14:20					TPJS 93
Malachi 1:2–3				Rom. 9:13–14	JS–Hist. 1:36–37; HC 4:262
Malachi 3–4		3 Ne. 24–25; 26:1			
Malachi 3:1			36:8; 45:9; 133:2	Matt. 11:10; Mark 1:2; Luke 7:21	
Malachi 3:2–3			13; 128:24		TPJS 173
Malachi 3:10					HBL Ensign, Nov. 71, p. 16
Malachi 3:17			101:3		
Malachi 4:1			29:9; 64:23–24; 133:64		JS–Hist. 1:37
Malachi 4:2		1 Ne. 22:15, 24; 2 Ne. 25:13; 26:4, 9			
Malachi 4:4					TPJS 322–323
Malachi 4:5–6			2; 27:9; 35:4; 98:16–17; 110:14–16; 128:17–18; 138:46–47		TPJS 160, 172, 321, 330, 337, 356

Sources Cited

Benson, Ezra Taft. *Conference Report* (Oct. 1988), p. 4.

Burton, Theodore M. *Conference Report* (Sept. 1967), p. 81.

———. Conference Report (Oct. 1970), p. 35.

Buttrick, George A., ed. *The Interpreter's Dictionary of the Bible*. Nashville, Tennessee: Abingdon Press, 1962.

Clark, James R., comp. *Messages of the First Presidency of The Church of Jesus Christ of Latter-day Saints*. 6 vols. Salt Lake City: Bookcraft, 1965–75.

Cowley, Matthias F. *Wilford Woodruff: History of His Life and Labors*. Salt Lake City: Bookcraft, 1964.

Gaster, Theodor H. *The Dead Sea Scriptures*. Garden City, NY: Anchor Books, 1964.

Hinckley, Gordon B. *Conference Report* (Apr. 1982), p. 60

Journal of Discourses, 26 vols. London: Latter-day Saints' Book Depot, 1854–86.

Kimball, Spencer W. *Conference Report* (Oct. 1947), p. 22.

———. *Conference Report* (April 1964), pp. 93–94.

———. *Ensign* (Dec. 1975), p. 4.

Kitto, John, Ed. *The Cyclopaedia of Biblical Literature*. 10th ed. 2 vols. New York: Ivison & Newman, 1853.

Lee, Harold B. *Ensign* (Nov. 1971), p. 15.

———. *Ensign* (Nov. 1971), p. 16.

McConkie, Bruce R. *The Millennial Messiah*. Salt Lake City: Deseret Book Company, 1982.

————. *The Mortal Messiah*. 4 vols. Salt Lake City: Deseret Book Company, 1979–81.

————. *The Promised Messiah*. Salt Lake City: Deseret Book Company, 1978.

Nyman, Monte S. *Great Are the Words of Isaiah*. Salt Lake City: Bookcraft, 1980.

————. "A Second Gathering of Israel." *Doctrines for Exaltation* (Sperry Symposium 1989). Salt Lake City: Deseret Book Company, 1989.

Petersen, Mark E. *Conference Report* (Apr. 1978), p. 95.

————. *Conference Report* (Apr. 1983), p. 43.

Rasmussen, Ellis T. *An Introduction to the Old Testament and Its Teachings*. Part 2. Provo, UT: Brigham Young University Press, 1967.

Richards, LeGrand. *Conference Report* (Oct. 1975), p. 75.

Roberts, B. H. *A Comprehensive History of the Church of Jesus Christ of Latter-day Saints, Century One*, 6 vols. Salt Lake City: The Church of Jesus Christ of Latter-day Saints, 1930.

Skousen, W. Cleon. *The Fourth Thousand Years*. Salt Lake City: Bookcraft, 1966.

Smith, Joseph Fielding. *Doctrines of Salvation*, 3 vols. Compiled by Bruce R. McConkie. Salt Lake City: Bookcraft, 1954–56.

Smith, Lucy Mack. *History of Joseph Smith by His Mother*. Reprint. Salt Lake City: Bookcraft, 1954.

Sperry, Sidney B. *The Voice of Israel's Prophets*. Salt Lake City: Deseret Book Company, 1952.

Smith, Joseph. *Teachings of the Prophet Joseph Smith*. Selected by Joseph Fielding Smith. Salt Lake City: Deseret Book Company, 1938.

Wirthlin, Joseph B. *Conference Report* (Oct. 1955), p. 155.

Index

Aaronic Priesthood, restoration of,
140–41
Abinadi, 33 n. 6
Abrahamic covenant, 7, 25–26,
58
Agency, 125
Ahab, king of Israel, 24
Ahaz, king of Judah, 77
Altar, sacred, of Bethel, 52
Amaziah, 55
America: as Zion, 11, 37, 66, 81,
115 n. 5; as holy mountain,
115; given to Joseph's
descendants, 115 n. 3
Ammon, 48
Amon, king of Judah, 92
Amos, 8; superscription dating
book of, 47; central theme of,
48; seven nations rebuked by,
48–49; visions of, 54–55,
56–57; calling of, 55
Angels: destruction of wicked by,
38, 144; Zechariah's vision of,
on horses, 123
Apocrypha, 97 n. 3
Apostasy: Amos's prophecy of, 56;

of Ten Tribes, 97; Nahum's
prophecy of, 98; brought about
by foolish shepherds, 132
Application versus interpretation
of scriptures, 36 n. 1, 42
Armageddon, battle of, 133
Assyrian captivity of Israel, 7–8,
13; prophesied by Amos, 17;
prophesied by Joel, 36;
prophesied by Micah, 78;
prophesied by Zechariah, 131

Baal, pagan god, 16, 23–24;
temple prostitutes of, 49
Babylon: spiritual, destruction of,
66; as fish that swallowed
Jonah, 71; latter-day, to lay
siege to Zion, 82–83
Babylonian captivity of Judah,
8–9, 71, 94, 100–101, 117
Baptism: for the dead, 67; among
Judah, 133
Benson, Ezra Taft, 66 n. 4
Bethlehem, 82–83
Book of law found by Josiah,
93–94

157

to, 2; Micah compared with, 77–78, 89–90

Israel: fall of, prophets foretold and witnessed, 2; covenants of, with God, 6–7, 50; Assyrian captivity of, 7–8; Babylonian captivity of, 8–9; ripened in iniquity, 14–15, 29; rejected warnings of prophets, 15–16; four sins of, mentioned by Amos, 49–50; Latter-day Saints as descendants of, 58; reuniting of tribes of, 59; Micah urges, to trust Lord, 88–89; stiffneckedness of, 121; to recognize Christ, 133. *See also* Gathering of Israel; Scattering of Israel; Ten Tribes of Israel

Jackson County, Missouri, 79, 80–81

Jacob, brother of Nephi, 121

Jacob, father of house of Israel, 33, 137–38

Jehoahaz, king of Judah, 94, 100

Jehoiakim, king of Judah, 94, 100–101

Jehosaphat, valley of, 43

Jehu, 24

Jeremiah: foreordination of, 3; quotations from, in New Testament, 4; fulfillment of prophecies of, 8–9; similarities between Obadiah and, 63–64; dating of, 109–10; prophesies of the BRANCH, 125

Jeroboam, king of Israel, 16, 22–23, 24 n. 3, 47

Jerusalem: gathering to, 39, 44, 109, 128–29; water flowing from under temple of, 45, 134–35;

gospel to be preached in, 80; conquest of, Habakkuk as witness of, 101; temple to be built in, 123; future of, shown to Zechariah, 124; Lord promises to dwell in, 128; all people gathered against, 132–33; identifying, as holy city, 135

Jesus Christ: commanded Nephites to search Isaiah's words, 1; quoted writings of prophets, 4; prophets testified of, 5; spoke of fulfillment of prophets, 5; as David, 28; to reign in Zion, 81; Micah prophesies of, 82–83; quotes prophecies of Micah, 83–87; Jews to believe in, 109, 133; as primary subject of Zechariah, 121; two comings of, confusing, 121; as BRANCH, 125, 127; to ride colt into Jerusalem, 129–30; betrayal of, by Judas, 132; to stand on mount of Olives, 134; sign given Nephites of birth of, 134; quoted Malachi, 136; messenger to prepare way of, 139–40; appearance of, in Kirtland Temple, 140; to arise with healing in wings, 145

Jewels of Lord, 143

Jezreel, 24

Joel, 8; passage from, quoted by Moroni, 35, 40; difficulty of dating, 35–36; intended audience of, 36; prophesies of apostasy and destruction of Israel, 37; prophesies of Second Coming of Christ, 37–39;